Event Code Uncovered

Secrets Buried in Sacred Text

More Historical Events Revealed Encoded in the Hebrew Torah, the Five Books of Moses, a 3400-Year-Old Text

Steve Canada

Author of:

(1) Bible-Encoded Crop Circle Gods (4 alien mysteries solved).

(2) Foretold in Sacred Code (all of history found encoded in the Torah).

(3) Death's Bible Code (accidents, assassinations, holocaust, mass shootings, natural disasters, terror attacks, wars – shown in Torah Matrices).

(4) End of Days 2014-2018 (adjusted Gregorian Calendar shows timeframe).

(5) Heaven and Hell Are Full, Angels of All Religions Returning at End of Days, AD 2014-2018 – names shown in Torah Matrices.

(6) Celebrities and Movie Stars Death Bible Code, Vol.1: Their Deadly Diseases and Names Shown in Torah Matrices.

(7) Celebrities and Movie Stars Death Bible Code, Vol.2: Their Fatal Cancers and Names Shown in Torah Matrices.

(8) Celebrities and Movie Stars Death Bible Code, Vol.3: Their Deaths by Accidents, Murders, Overdoses, and Suicides … and Names Shown in Torah Matrices.

authorHOUSE®

AuthorHouse™
1663 Liberty Drive
Bloomington, IN 47403
www.authorhouse.com
Phone: 1 (800) 839-8640

Published by AuthorHouse 05/14/2015

ISBN: 978-1-5049-0821-4 (sc)
ISBN: 978-1-5049-0853-5 (e)

Print information available on the last page.

Any people depicted in stock imagery provided by Thinkstock are models,
and such images are being used for illustrative purposes only.
Certain stock imagery © Thinkstock.

This book is printed on acid-free paper.

Contents

Preface

Death rears its ugly head everywhere and at all times, in all sorts of situations and under many kinds of circumstances and fro a myriad of reasons, affecting people in surprising ways, but eventually coming for everyone no matter their station in life. But why do we find their demises encoded in the Five Books of Moses? What is it about a sacred text of 304,805 Hebrew letters that enables it to hold the whole history of humankind, and encoded within it the specific circumstances under which particular people have died or are going to die?

Connected to the types of events listed in this book are found the names of those who died in instances of those particular events, except in Part 6 where only the historical political facts are found encoded, since the deaths of those named were not searched for in the Torah, but might be in a future book.

The Jewish people gave the world the Eternal Book of Books, the original text of which, the Torah, is used here to explore some of what might be hidden in it. The 'Bible Codes Plus' computer program used also contains the original text of the larger *Tanach*, Books outside the Five Books of Moses, which also can be searched for hidden, encoded names and terms. The *Tanach* is made of the Torah, the Navi'im (Prophets), and Chetuvim (Writings) … all making up The Hebrew Bible, what Christians call the 'Old Testament.'

Introduction

"The only new thing in this world is the history you don't know." Harry Truman

Sections in this book are only representative samples of material that could be developed into full-length books. The Torah (the Five Books of Moses in what some call 'The Old Testament') is encoded with many interesting names and phrases, along with applicable dates, some apparently predictive of historical events, at least in a relative way, since the text is about 3400 years old. These are discovered by counting any certain number of letters, that is 'skipping' any detected number of letters (ELS … Equidistant Letter Sequence) starting from anywhere in the original Hebrew text. This search method was first discovered by rabbis about 900 years ago who noticed small patterns in the text they were reading.

Code searchers usually restrict their work to the Torah, the first five books of the Bible, that is from Genesis through Deuteronomy. My earlier book, *Death's Bible Code* (2013), found names of the dead throughout history, from ancient Egypt to Auschwitz to the Titanic to Sandy Hook mass shooting to Boston marathon bombing; and Assassinations over 4000 years, casualties of wars, accidents, mass shootings, natural disasters, and terror attacks – their names are found secretly encoded in the sacred Word of Yahweh, *with* the names of the event in which they died.

The embedded Torah information is clear, conspicuous and concise. The original Hebrew text seen in the chapters and sections of this book has not been changed even by *one* letter in about 3400 years, since the time Yahweh dictated it letter-by-letter to Moses on Mt. Sinai, according the Orthodox view. I don't know precisely who composed and dictated the Torah, or how much care, effort, time, resources or editing went into its design or code architecture, but given what has been uncovered in the plain text just by counting between letters during the past 900 years of Bible Code study, the nature of the intelligence behind it is consistent with what is known elsewhere about the identity and abilities of Yahweh (see Sitchin in References).

Search for terms entered is done automatically by the Bible Code program (for example, *Bible Codes Plus*, available from Israel via USPS). Search is done forward, then backward through the whole Torah or whole Tanach, the larger Hebrew Bible (or within any range you specify); any spelling direction found is valid, be it horizontal, vertical or diagonal. No knowledge of any Hebrew is needed in order to do Bible Code research. Search terms can be entered using the program's dictionary or lexicon or 'dates' list, or entered phonetically using transliteration (letter-by-letter, sound for corresponding sound from English to Hebrew using the program's on-screen keyboard).

The first term the program will search for is the 'Key,' and if found encoded it will stand vertically, with letters touching in correct spelling sequence, either top-to-bottom or the reverse. Any spelling direction of any searched-for term found encoded is a valid search result. When found encoded near the Key, the validity of the connection between the Key and such terms is revealed as part of the strength of the Bible Code itself. Up to six terms can be searched for at the same time, along with the Key.

'Proximity' means the visual distance between the Key Code and any other code or word in the retrieved Matrix. Bible Code research theory states that the closer the pairings are, i.e., the more compact the visual cluster effect, the greater their significance. Jeffrey Satinover, MD, in his book *Cracking the Bible Code*, says "there is a tendency for meaningfully related words to show the cluster effect, appearing in the array more closely together than unrelated words." (Quoted in manual on p.9 that comes with the *Bible Codes Plus* computer program on CD-ROM).

The essential sounds that comprise the encoded words are phonetically rendered coherent, readable and understandable through transliteration, finding the equivalent sound of the English letter in the appropriate, corresponding Hebrew letter that has the same sound as shown in the on-screen keyboard … those strung together in correct spelling sequence, keeps the English sound of the word entered in the search function of the program; for example 'Avalanche.'

The odds of the Key in any particular Matrix being found encoded by chance can go as low as one in a million or less as calculated automatically by the program. While the odds could be even lower than that, the program does not calculate below that. The encodement algorithm used by the Torah composers that allows such dense search results of the encoded found terms (whether in separate syllables or not) encoded so close to the Key (see important 'Proximity' note above) and to each other, is a function of an unknown technology and encryption mathematics.

Satinover points out that his contacts at the NSA have concluded that humans today do not have the computing, encryption, encoding power, or the mathematical knowledge, to encode such a large text to the deep extent as we see in the Torah when a Bible Code program is applied and terms searched for.

While it may be true that "some secrets should stay buried" (as the 10-part television series on USA channel, 'Dig,' says) here we have the opportunity to uncover secrets buried in a scared text for at least 3400 years. Whether or not such secrets shown in black and white in Torah Matrices in this book should not be revealed to the public will need to be judged by the reader.

Fig. 1

Hebrew Alphabet

Translation and Transliteration

Hebrew letter:	for English sound	as for example in:
Ayin ע =	a	
Aleph א	A or E	Around
Beth ב	B	Boston
Caph כ	C	Carnival
Daleth ד	D	Door
Aleph א	E	Energy
Peh פ	F	First
Gimmel ג	G	Grand
Heh ה	H	Hello
Yod י	I	Israel
Gimmel ג *or* Yod י	J	Jack
Kuf ק	K	Kennedy
Lamed ל	L	London
Mem מ	M	Mother
Nun נ	N	Never
Vav ו	O	mOre
Peh פ	P	Poor
Kuf ק	Q	Queen
Resh ר	R	Rank
Samech ס *or* Sin ש	S	Silence
Shin ש	Sh	Sugar
Tav ת	Th	THeater
Tet ט	T	theaTer
Vav ו	U	sUgar
Vav ו	V	Victory
Vav (*press twice*) וו	W	Window

Part 1

From Avalanches to Vatican Popes' Deaths Found Bible-Torah Encoded

Alphabetical List of Categories Searched For; most illustrated as Torah Matrices, as 'Figures' (listed here not in order). Those categories listed with no attached Figure have been found as a Key and are in various book-development stages of completion, either separately or together in a manuscript.

Avalanches (Fig.2),
Baseball (Fig.36),
Basketball (Figs. 37, 38),
Beheading (Figs.3-6D),
Boxing (Figs.45,46),
Bullfighting (Fig.47),
Diseases (in Part 3),
Floods
Football (Figs.39-41),
Forest Fires
Genocides
Grammy Award Winners (Fig.43),
Home Invasions
Hollywood Movie Oscars (Figs.31-35),
Hostages (Figs.11-13),
Hurricane (Fig.48),
Ice Hockey (Fig.49),
Mass Shooting (Figs.14-18),
Mining Disasters (Figs.19,20),
Mountain Climbing Accidents (Fig.21),
Mud-Land Slides
NASCAR
Nobel Prizes
Olympics (Fig.50),
Plane Crashes (Figs.22,23),
Pulitzer Prizes
Rebellions and Uprisings
Road-rage
Rollercoaster Deaths
Serial Killings

Soccerball (Fig.42),
Tennis (Fig.51),
Terror Attacks (Figs.24-26),
Tony Awards (Fig.44),
Train Crashes (Figs.27-30),
Vatican Popes' Deaths (Figs.7-10).

All of the above headings are essentially descriptive terms used as the Key for Torah Code Matrices in which are found encoded, related terms of the events or subject, including those who died. While most have examples shown in this book, some do not. Each could be expanded into a book-length manuscript, some of multiple volumes showing the complete history of the heading's topic.

Other sports, awards, and prizes will be searched for later, including championship winners of awards and prizes. To be included in a future book. As Torah Matrix illustrations, see Figures 2 to 51 on the following pages. The earlier Figure 1 is the Hebrew Alphabet and its letter sounds, for equivalence in transliteration into English, as shown in many Torah Code Matrices used in this book.

Fig. 2

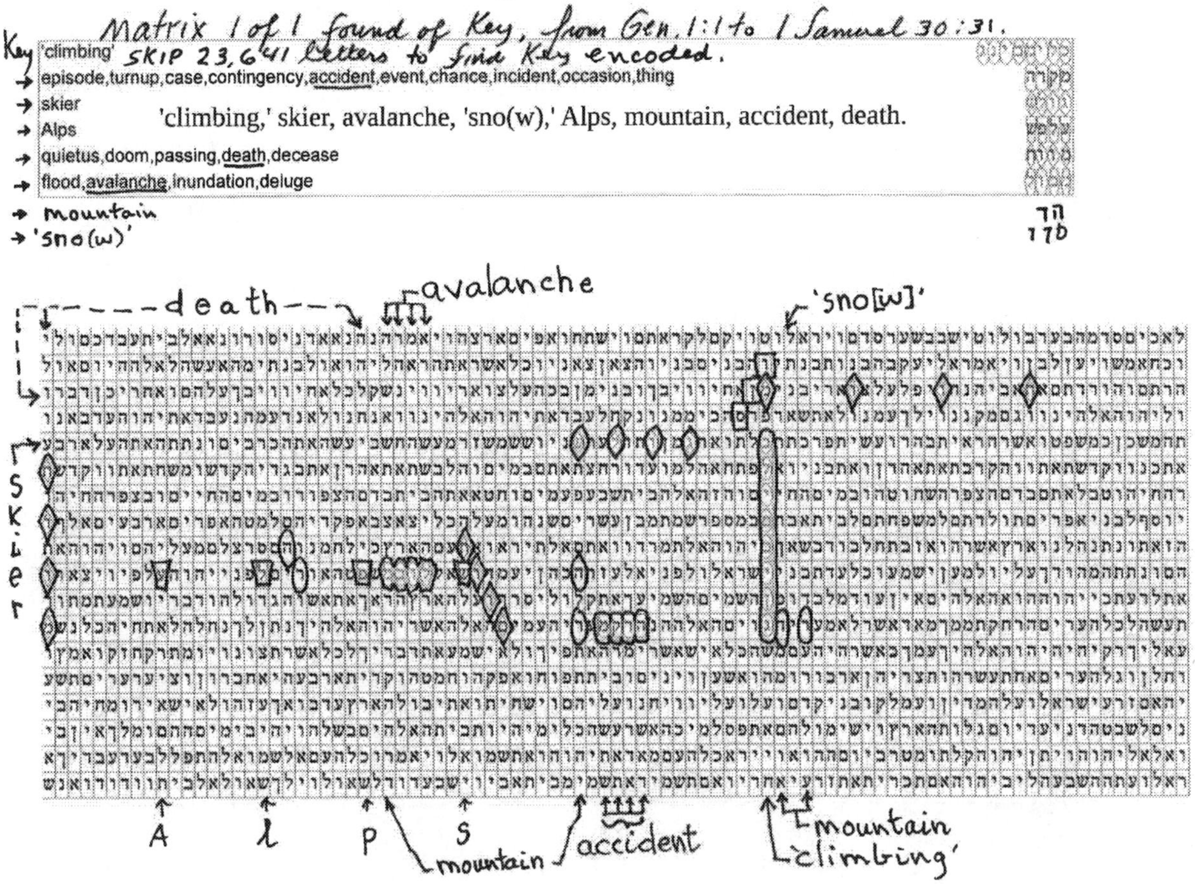

Matrix 1 of 1 found of Key, from Gen. 1:1 to 1 Samuel 30:31.

Key 'climbing' SKIP 23,641 letters to find Key encoded.

→ episode,turnup,case,contingency,accident,event,chance,incident,occasion,thing

→ skier   'climbing,' skier, avalanche, 'sno(w),' Alps, mountain, accident, death.

→ Alps

→ quietus,doom,passing,death,decease

→ flood,avalanche,inundation,deluge

→ mountain

→ 'sno(w)'

The Key, 'climbing,' is phonetically transliterated into Hebrew
letters sounds, as is 'sno.'

Fig. 3

Matrix 1 of 1 found of Key, from Gen. 44:16 to 1 Samuel 17:46. SKIP 17,331 letters to find Key encoded.

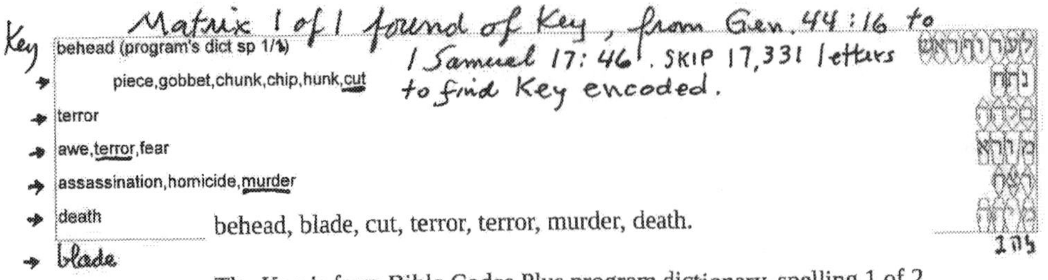

Key

behead (program's dict sp 1/2)

piece, gobbet, chunk, chip, hunk, cut

terror

awe, terror, fear

assassination, homicide, murder

death

blade

behead, blade, cut, terror, terror, murder, death.

The Key is from Bible Codes Plus program dictionary, spelling 1 of 2.
More could be labeled here and to right and left of this screen print.

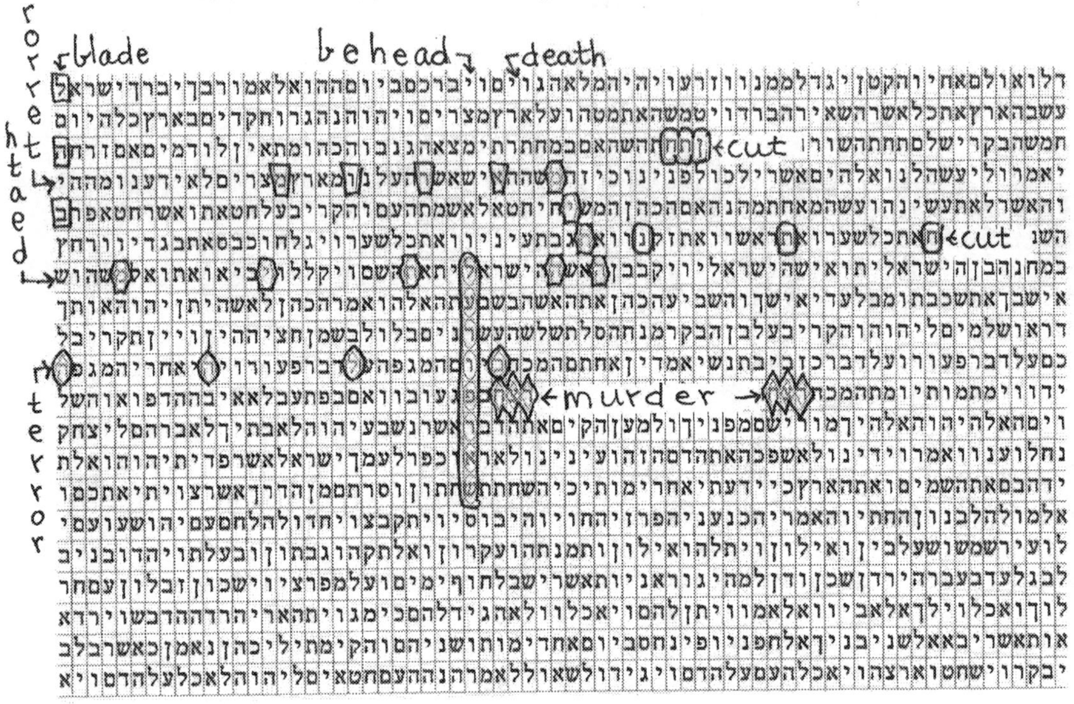

Fig. 4

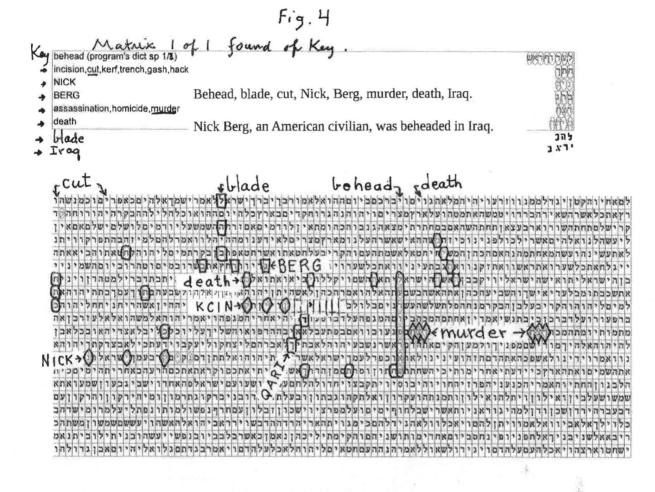

Matrix 1 of 1 found of Key.

Key: behead (program's dict sp 1/1)
incision,cut,kerf,trench,gash,hack
NICK
BERG
assassination,homicide,murder
death
blade
Iraq

Behead, blade, cut, Nick, Berg, murder, death, Iraq.

Nick Berg, an American civilian, was beheaded in Iraq.

The 2 'terror' spellings are also encoded here; see Figure 3.
More 'blade' could be labeled here but they're not highlighted.
Only one of phonetic 'Iraq' is found encoded here.

Fig. 5

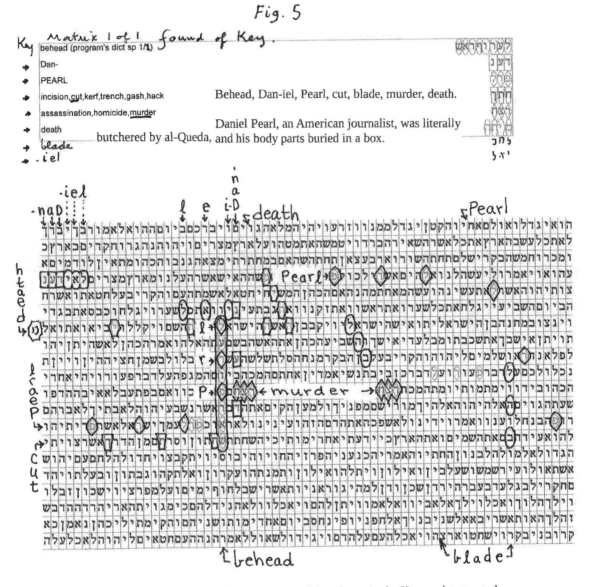

Behead, Dan-iel, Pearl, cut, blade, murder, death.

Daniel Pearl, an American journalist, was literally butchered by al-Queda, and his body parts buried in a box.

Note Hebrew spelling of 'Pearl' (consonants only), 'prl,' are in the Key, each separated by one letter. No more intimate association with historical reality is possible in this instance. The Torah encoders had access to an inescapable truth that locks out fate with the sound of Yahweh's words.

Fig. 6

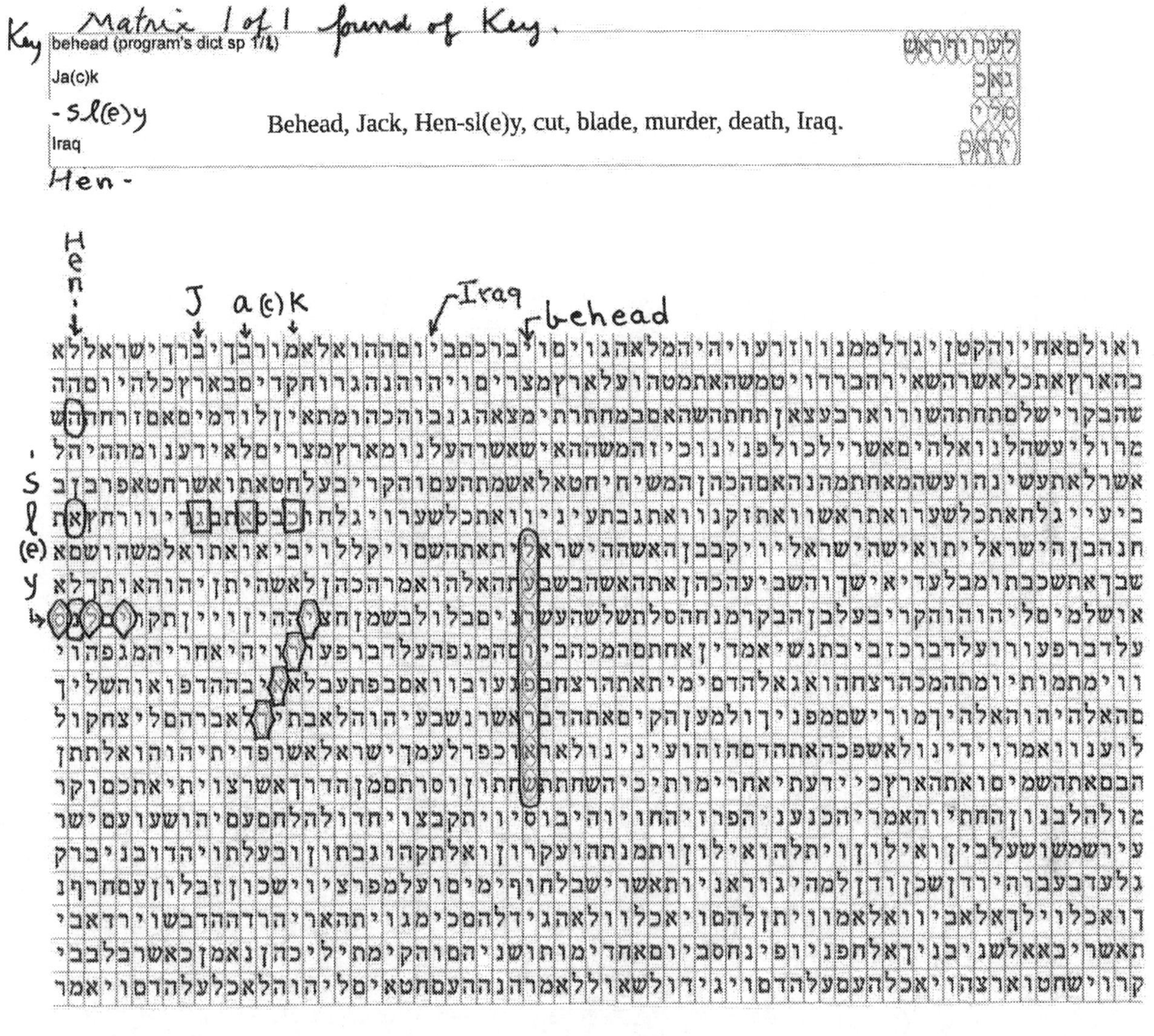

behead (program's dict sp 1/1)

Ja(c)k

-sl(e)y

Iraq

Hen-

לעשרי ח(ד)ראש
נאכ
ילע(י)
ירואש

Behead, Jack, Hen-sl(e)y, cut, blade, murder, death, Iraq.

Hen-
J a(c)K   -Iraq   -behead
Hen-
-S
l
(e)
y

Jack Hensley, an American engineer, was beheaded in Iraq on Sept. 21, 2004.
Date was not found encoded here. More '-sl(e)y' could be labeled here, but they're
not highlighted. See prior Figures for location of "cut, blade, murder, death."

Fig. 6-A

SKIP 17,331 letters to find Key encoded.

Key
behead (program's dict sp 1/1)
→ Cop-
→ Libya
→ Isis
→ egyptian
→ February
      - tic
→ 21   X 3
→ christ, Jesus יש׳

Behead, Libya, ISIS, February [Shvat], Egyptian, Cop-tic, Christ(ian), 21.

21 Egyptian migrants, Coptic Christian men, in Libya working and looking for work, were beheaded on a beach in or near Derna, Libya, on the northeast coast.

Part 2 → (below)

- Part 1 -

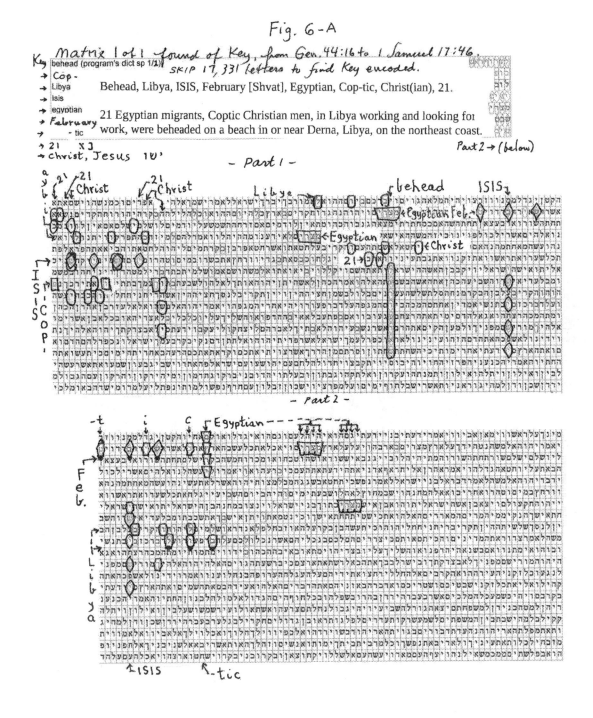

- Part 2 -

Fig. 6-B

Matrix 1 of 1 found of Key, from Gen 44:16 to 1 Samuel 17:46.
SKIP 17,331 letters to find Key encoded.

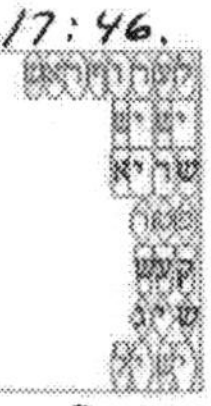

Key
behead (program's dict sp 1/2)
→ Isis
→ 'S(y)ria'
→ P(e)t(e)r
→ Kas-
→ -Sig-
→ ISIL
→ Nov [ember]

Behead, S(y)ria, Peter, Kas-sig, ISIS, ISIL, 'Nov'[ember].
The year, 2014, not found encoded here. More 'Nov' could be labeled.
Peter Kassig, 26, an American murdered by 'Jihad John', a Brit from
East London, in Syria. Kassig was taken captive in Oct. 2013, and con-
verted to Islam. He was a U.S. Army Ranger turned aid worker in Syria.

Part 2 → (below)

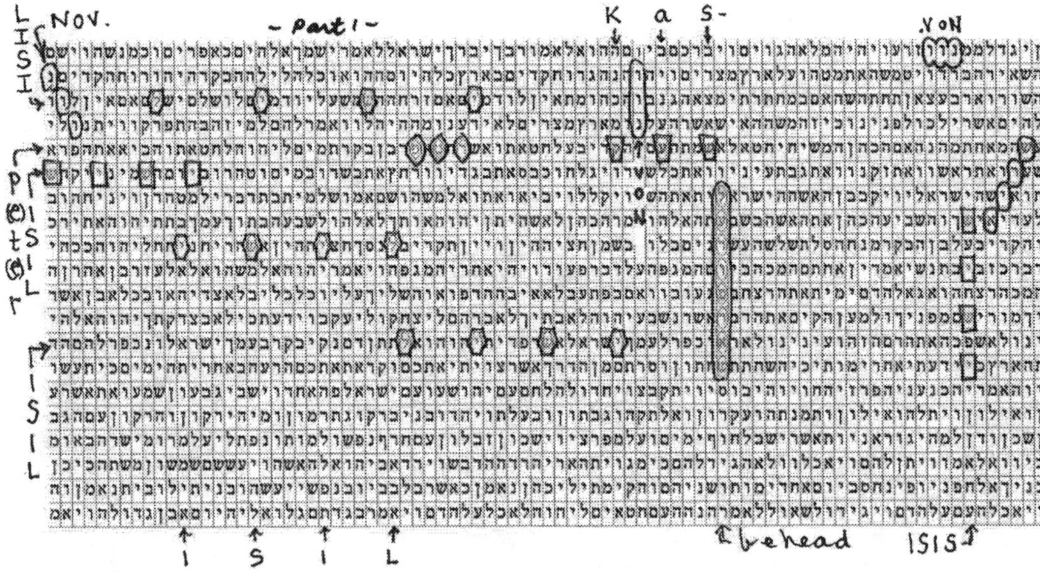

Fig. 6-C

Matrix 1 of 1 found of Key.

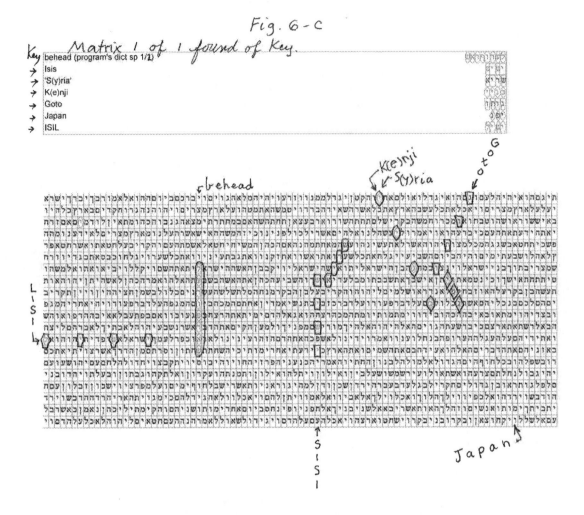

Behead, K(e)nji, Goto, Japan, ISIS, ISIL, Syria.
Goto, age 47, husband and father of 3, Japanese freelance journalist, captured in
October, 2014; video released on January 31, 2015; date of beheading unknown.

Fig. 6-D

Matrix 1 of 1 found of Key

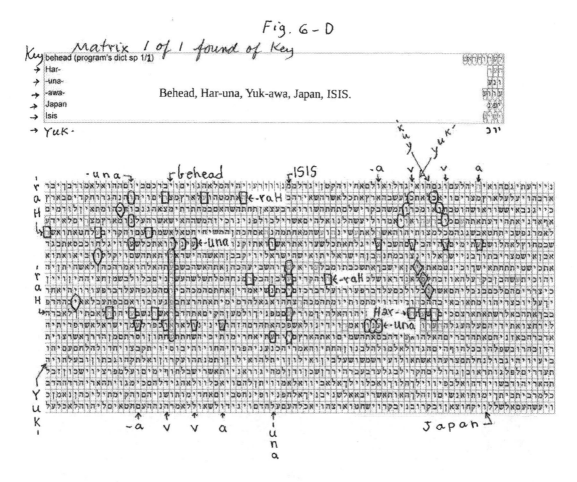

Behead, Har-una, Yuk-awa, Japan, ISIS.

Haruna Yukawa, Japanese, was in Syria trying to start a security company.
He was beheaded on about January 24, 2015, by ISIS.

Fig. 7

Matrix 13 of 17 found of Key, from Exodus 5:4 to Numbers 20:2. SKIP 7022 to find Key encoded.

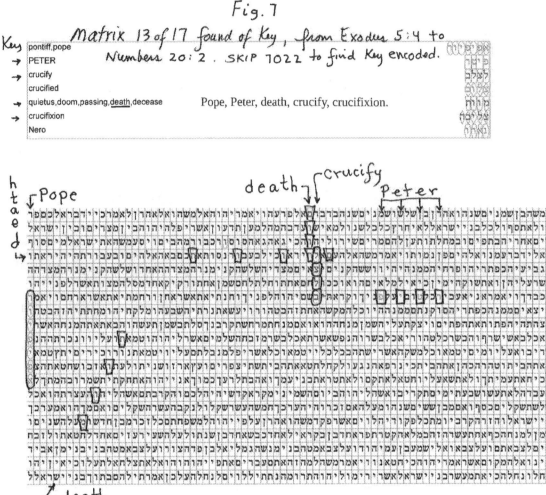

Pope, Peter, death, crucify, crucifixion.

'Pope' is program's dictionary spelling 1 of 1.
'Peter,' the first pope, is from program's First Names list.
'Death' is dictionary's spelling 2 of 2.
'Crucify' is dictionary's spelling 1 of 2.
'Crucifixion' is dictionary's spelling 2 of 2 and is left of the Key 37 columns
(vertical, 1-skip). He died during Nero's reign of terror, between 64 and 68AD.
While 'Nero' isn't found encoded in this Matrix 13 of 17 of Key ('Pope'),
'Nero' is found in 11 of the 17 Matrices.

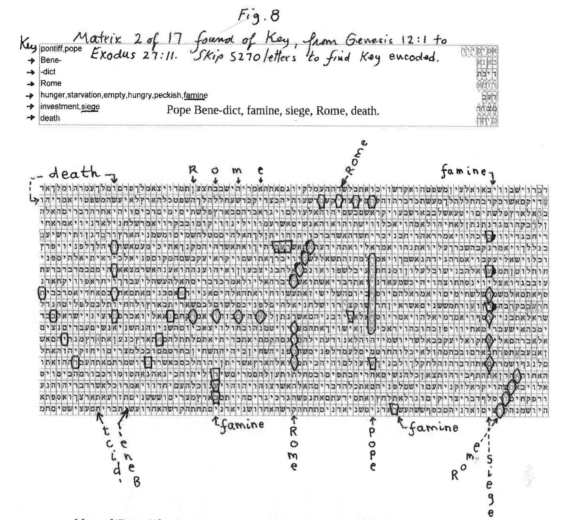

Fig. 8

Matrix 2 of 17 found of Key, from Genesis 12:1 to Exodus 27:11. Skip 5270 letters to find Key encoded.

Key
pontiff, pope
→ Bene-
→ -dict
→ Rome
→ hunger, starvation, empty, hungry, peckish, famine
→ investment, siege
→ death

Pope Bene-dict, famine, siege, Rome, death.

More of 'Rome,' 'famine,' 'siege,' and 'death' are to the right of this screen print.
Pope Benedict I died during the siege of Rome in 579AD, from famine.

Fig. 9

Matrix 2 of 17 found of Key, from Genesis 12:1 to
Exodus 27:11. SKIP 5270 letters to find Key encoded.

Key
pontiff, pope
→ Silv(e)-
→ -rius
→ exile, knob, stud, pommel, node, expatriate, Exile
→ hunger, starvation, empty, hungry, peckish, famine
starved
→ death

Pope, Silv(e)-rius, exile, starvation, death.

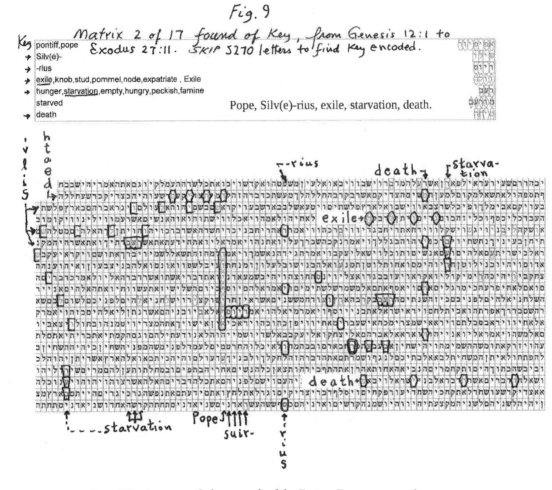

Pope Silverius was exiled as a result of the Eastern Roman emperor's
scheming, and died in 337AD of starvation.
'starvation' is from dictionary's spelling 1 of 1.

Fig. 10

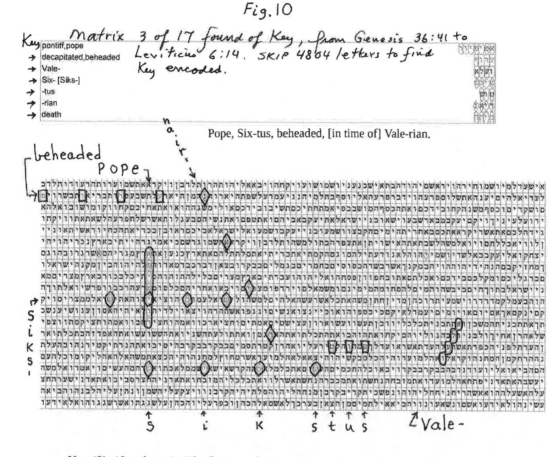

Matrix 3 of 17 found of Key, from Genesis 36:41 to Leviticus 6:14. skip 4864 letters to find Key encoded.

Key:
- pontiff, pope
- decapitated, beheaded
- Vale-
- Six- [Siks-]
- -tus
- -rian
- death

Pope, Six-tus, beheaded, [in time of] Vale-rian.

Note 'Six-' [as phonetic 'Siks-'] crosses the Key and even shares a letter, i, with it. To left 55 columns is 'death,' vertical, 1-letter-skip.

Pope Sixtus II was decapitated, along with four senior churchmen, in the time of Valerian. He ruled in 257-58AD. There have been about 264 popes in all, up to 2015. The diseases and causes of deaths of these popes, as found in the Bible Code, are the subject of a forthcoming book by the author.

Fig. 11

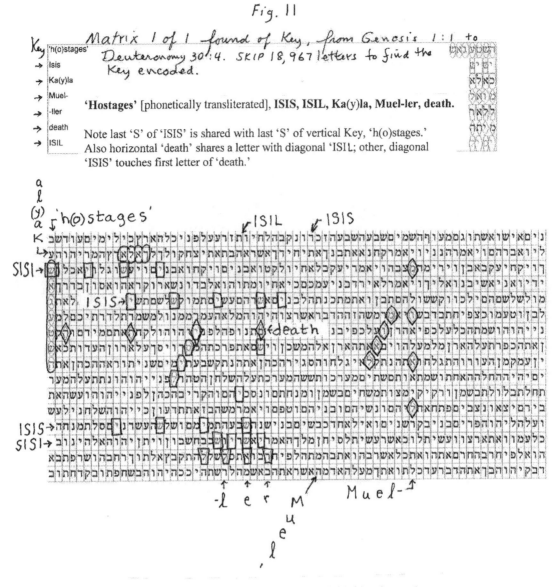

Matrix 1 of 1 found of Key, from Genesis 1:1 to Deuteronomy 30:4. SKIP 18,967 letters to find the Key encoded.

'Hostages' [phonetically transliterated], **ISIS, ISIL, Ka(y)la, Muel-ler, death.**

Note last 'S' of 'ISIS' is shared with last 'S' of vertical Key, 'h(o)stages.'
Also horizontal 'death' shares a letter with diagonal 'ISIL; other, diagonal
'ISIS' touches first letter of 'death.'

Her first name in upper left touches an 'S' of horizontal 'ISIS' ... the touch
of death in her case.
In bottom center note the last part of her name ('-ler') touches <u>all 4 letters</u> of 'ISIS.'

Fig. 12

Matrix 1 of 1 found of Key, from Gen. 1:1 to Deut. 30:4
SKIP 18,967 letters to find Key encoded.

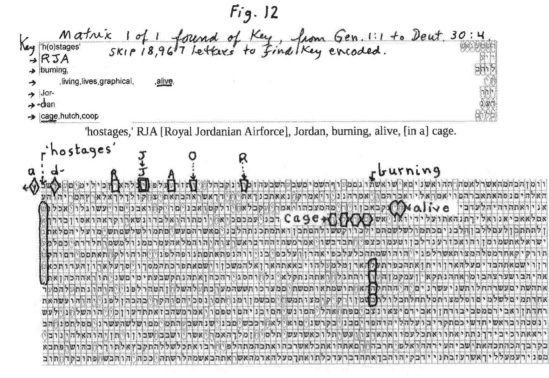

'hostages,' RJA [Royal Jordanian Airforce], Jordan, burning, alive, [in a] cage.

Royal Jordanian Airforce pilot, Muath al-Kassasbeth, was burned alive on January 3, 2015 in a cage. He was one of the hostages of ISIS. See Fig.13 for his name found encoded.

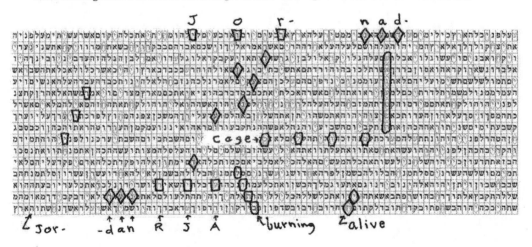

Fig. 13

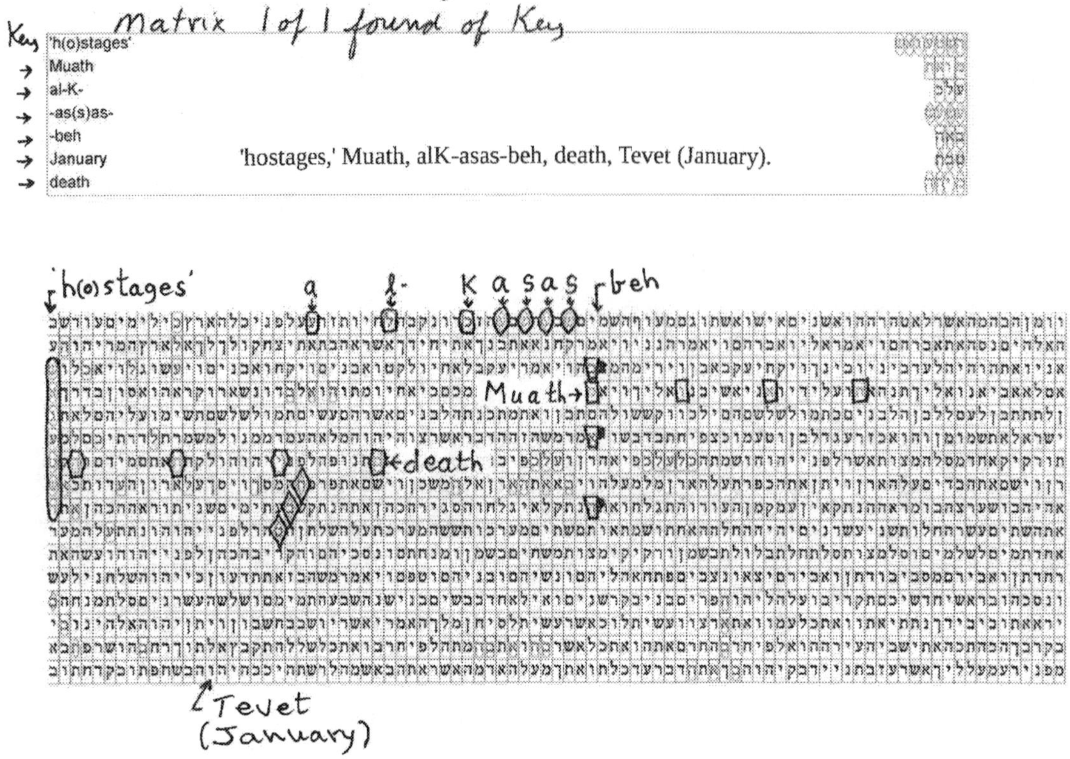

matrix 1 of 1 found of Key

Key
- 'h(o)stages'
- → Muath
- → al-K-
- → -as(s)as-
- → -beh
- → January
- → death

'hostages,' Muath, alK-asas-beh, death, Tevet (January).

'h(o)stages' a l- K a s a s beh

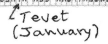

Muath →

death

[Tevet
(January)

Fig. 14

Part B ⟶

Matrix 1 of 1 found of the Key, from Exodus 36:14 to Deuteronomy 18:4. SKIP 7405 letters to find Key encoded.

— Part A —

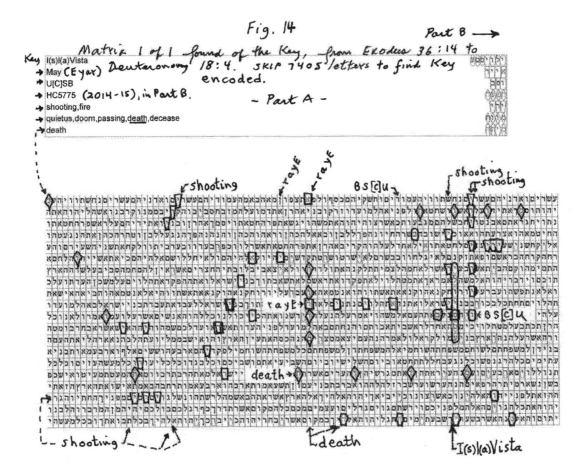

Key
- I(s)I(a)Vista
- May (Eyar)
- U[C]SB
- HC5775 (2014-15), in Part B.
- shooting, fire
- quietus, doom, passing, death, decease
- death

Isla Vista
I(s)l(a)Vista, U[C]SB, May [Eyar], HC5775 (2014-15),
shooting, death, death

Fig. 15

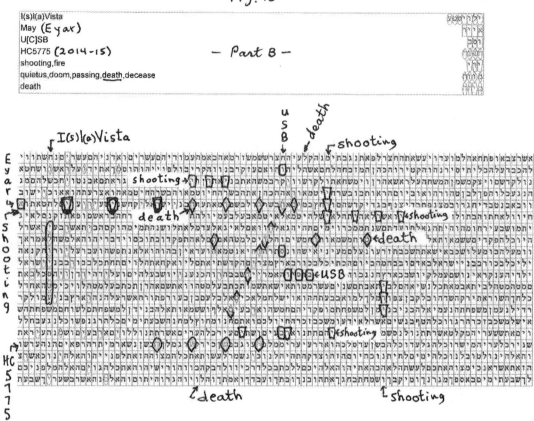

- Part B -

In center, note diagonal 2-way encoding of 'death,' done so elegantly they don't even share a letter. Note a 'USB' crossing them vertically, and the year Hebrew Calendar year (HC5775) near bottom almost touches 'death' and 'shooting.'

In upper left, note month (Eyar, May) and 'shooting' share 3 letters, and is so close to 'death' and the vertical Key, the location of the shooting death(s) in May of 2014.

Fig. 16

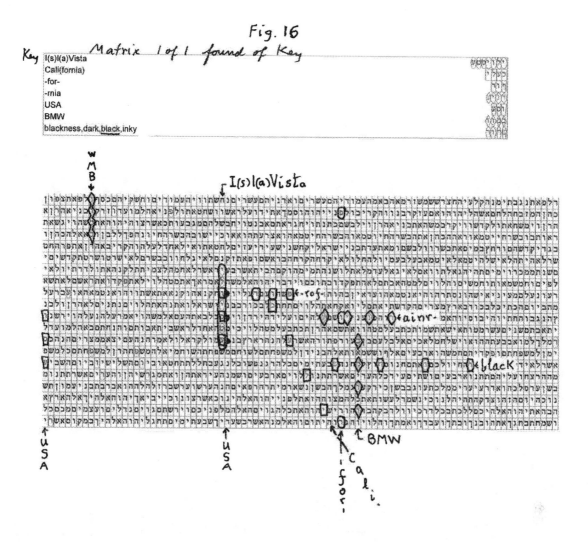

I(s)l(a)Vista, Cali-for-nia; USA; BMW, black.
E. Rodger drove a black BMW as he shot his gun
and also ran down the bicyclist.

Fig. 17

Matrix 1 of 1 found of Key

IlVista, Ell-iot, Rod-ger, unstable, delusion.

Key: l(s)l(a)Vista
Ell-
-iot
RODD, ROD -
-ger
unstable,dicky,shaky,ramshackle,unsound,dilapidated,decrepit
fantasy,phantasy,delusion

More Ell-iot could be labeled here. Note in upper right, the -d- of his last name
<u>touches</u> a letter of 'delusion' in encoded Hebrew (horizontal, on row 2). And
his first name is only 6 rows below, spelled out and touching all on one row.

His last name brackets the Key; his first name share a letter with it. Even
the fact that he was 'unstable' (Hebrew word of 4 letters) even shares a letter
-a- with the vertical Key.

Fig. 18

Alpha Phi Sorority, death.

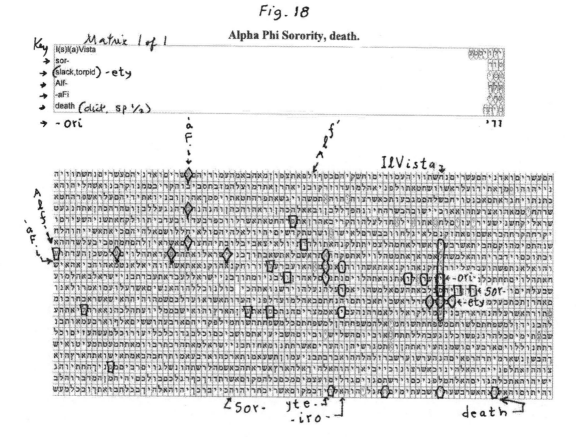

IlVista, Alf-aFi; Sor-ori-ety; death.
While 'ety' means something in Hebrew, we take only the phonetic
here as part of standard practice in Bible Code research.
More '-ori-' could be labeled here. And we know where 'shooting'
is found encoded.

Fig. 19

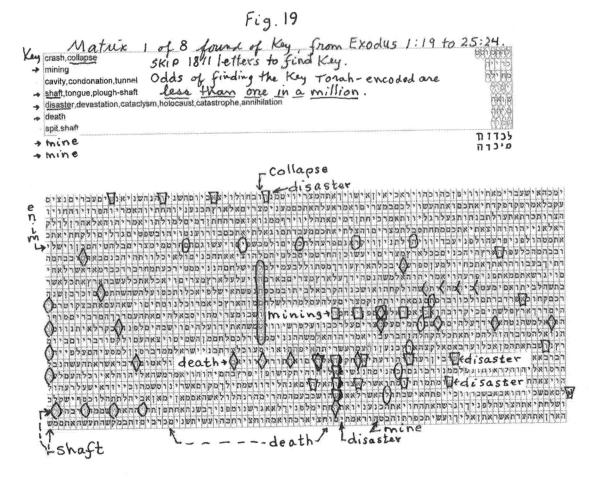

Collapse, mining, shaft, mine, disaster, death, mine.

In lower center, on row 6 from bottom, notice the shared letter of horizontal 'death' and 'disaster.' And 4 rows above that note the diagonal 'death' shares a letter with horizontal 'mining.'

Fig. 20

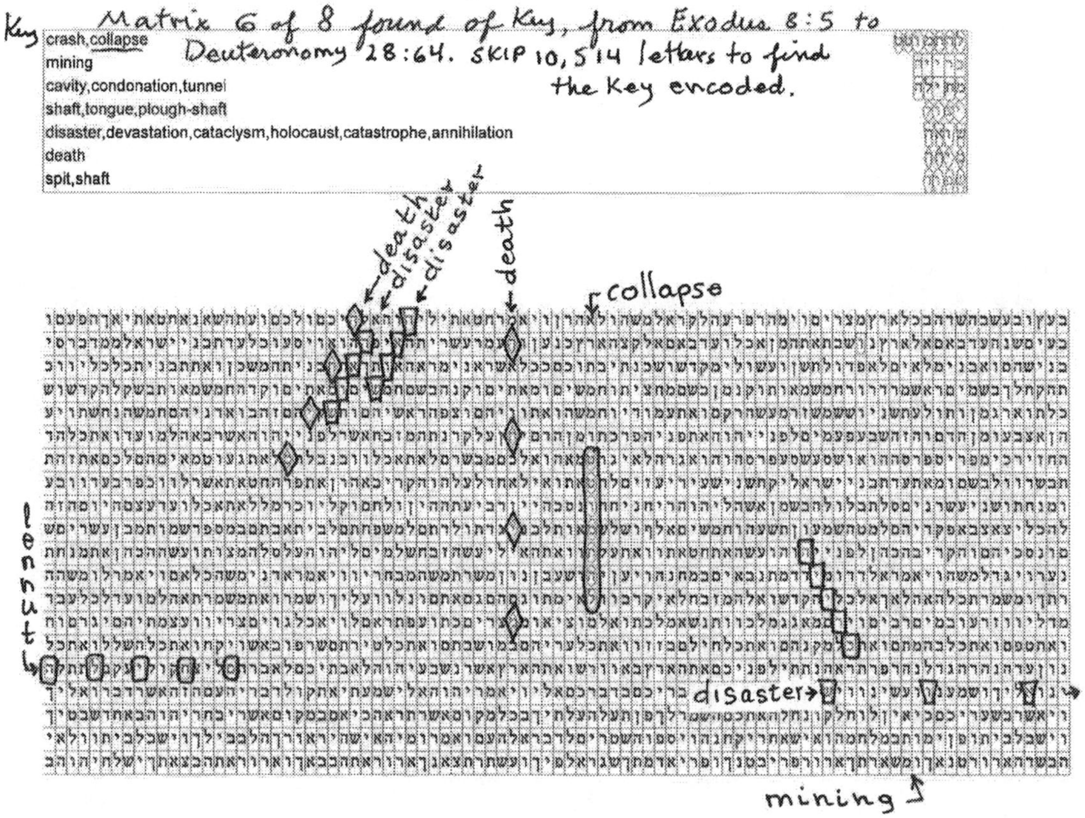

collapse, mining, tunnel, disaster, death.

The whole history of mining disasters and deaths could be found encoded in these 8 Torah Matrices, including location of the mine, and names of those who died in those accidents. This might comprise a lengthy book.

Fig. 21

Matrix 1 of 1 found of Key, from Gen. 1:1 to 1 Samuel 30:31.

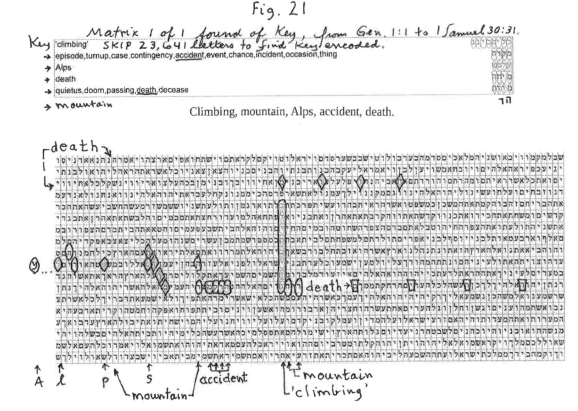

Climbing, mountain, Alps, accident, death.

Other names of mountain ranges around the world would be found encoded in this Matrix.
Many more 2-lettered 'mountain' could be labeled here.
The Key, 'climbing,' is transliterated.

Dictionary spelling 3 of 3 of 'mountaineer' and its search finds 12 encoded at its maximum search skip of 43,543 letters, that is, 12 different Matrices would be found, each with its own maximum skip search results. So a history of mountaineering and resulting deaths could be found Torah-encoded, and is to comprise a copyrighted full-length book in progress by the author.

Fig. 22

Matrix 1 of 1 found of Key, from Gen. 42:11 to Deut. 13:19.

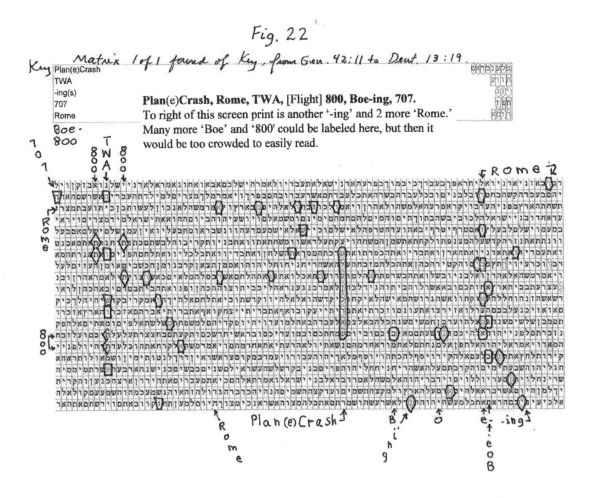

Plan(e)Crash, Rome, TWA, [Flight] 800, Boe-ing, 707.
To right of this screen print is another '-ing' and 2 more 'Rome.'
Many more 'Boe' and '800' could be labeled here, but then it
would be too crowded to easily read.

**Rome, Italy, November 23, 1964, TWA Flight 800, Boeing
707 crashed on takeoff, 50 of the 73 aboard were killed.**

Fig. 23

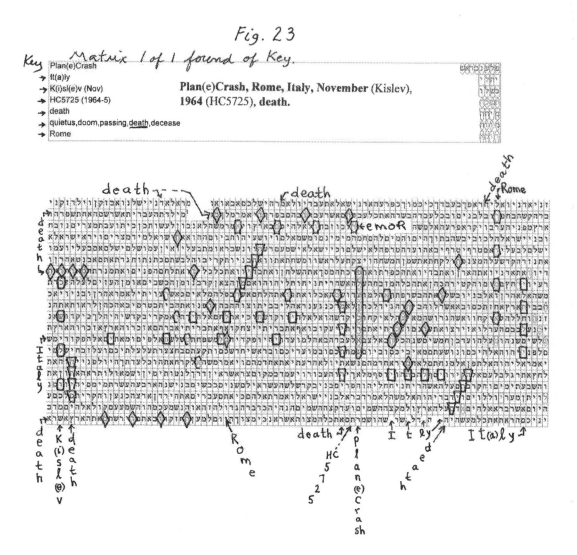

To right of this screen print are 3 more 'death,' 3 more 'Rome,' 2 more 'Italy' and 1 more 'HC5725.' Redundancy is the hallmark of good communication, and the Torah encoders are very good communicators.

Fig. 24

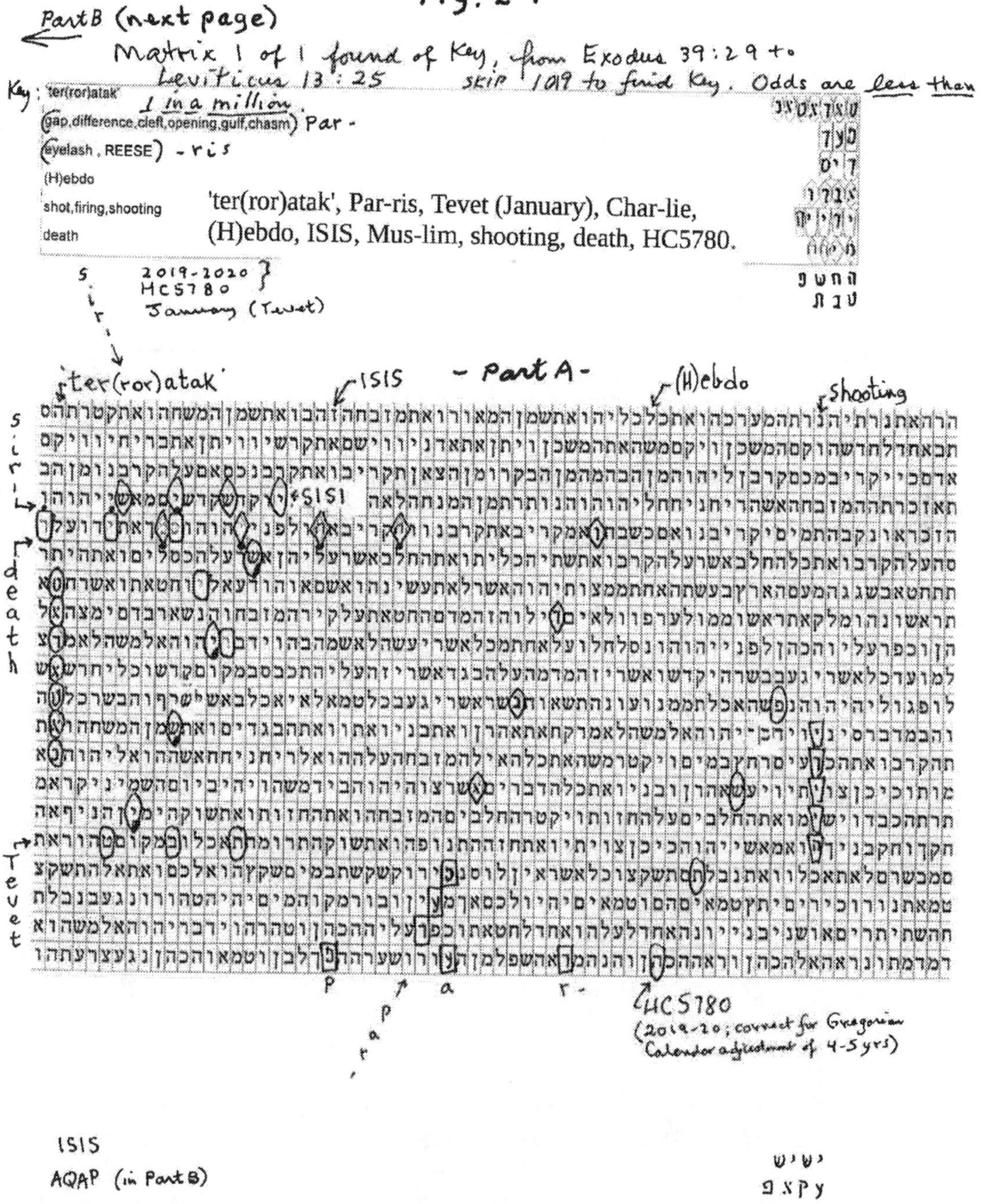

PartB (next page)

Matrix 1 of 1 found of Key, from Exodus 39:29 to Leviticus 13:25 skip 1019 to find Key. Odds are less than 1 in a million.

Key: 'ter(ror)atak'
(gap,difference,cleft,opening,gulf,chasm) Par-
(eyelash, REESE) -ris
(H)ebdo
shot,firing,shooting
death

'ter(ror)atak', Par-ris, Tevet (January), Char-lie, (H)ebdo, ISIS, Mus-lim, shooting, death, HC5780.

s
i
r

2019-2020 }
HC5780 }
January (Tevet)

'ter(ror)atak'   ISIS   - Part A -   (H)ebdo   Shooting

s
i
r
i
l
death

Tevet

P   a   r
P
a
r

HC5780
(2019-20; correct for Gregorian
Calendar adjustment of 4-5 yrs)

ISIS

AQAP (in Part B)

While the month found encoded is correct, the year, 2019-20, can be seen as adjusted according to Gregorian Calendar correction needed, as explained in the Appendix. Odds of finding the Key encoded in the Torah at a search skip of 1019 letters are less than one in a million against pure chance. 'AQAP' is found encoded in Part B.

Fig. 25

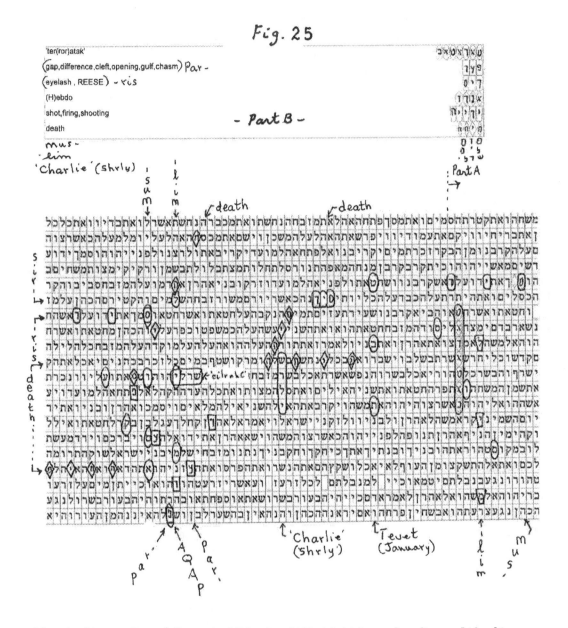

'ter(ror)atak'

(gap,difference,cleft,opening,gulf,chasm) Par-

(eyelash , REESE) ~ ris

(H)ebdo

shot,firing,shooting

death

- Part B -

mus-
-lim
'Charlie' (Shrly)

Note in this Part B, on left, vertical 'Mus-' and '-lim' (which touches diagonal 'death' **and** <u>shares</u> last letter of 'Charly'). On right, diagonal 'Mus-' touches and crosses the Key. More 'Mus-' and 'lim' could be labeled here. Another ISIS is here but is obscured by 'Charlie', horizontal on row 11, sharing 2 letters with it. 'AQAP' [al-Queda in the Arabian Peninsula] is in lower left, diagonal, and shares the 'P' of 'Par-.'

Fig. 26

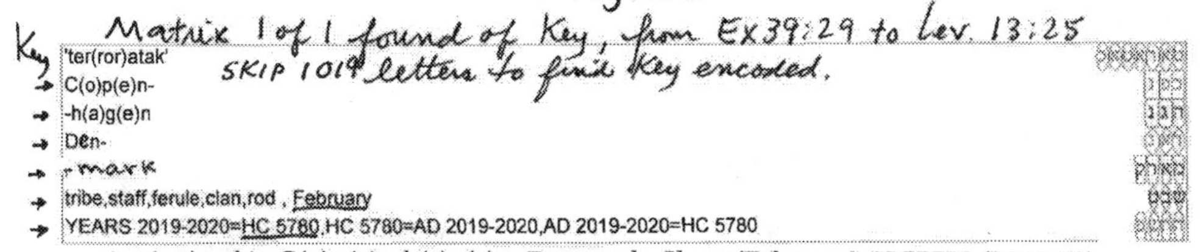

Matrix 1 of 1 found of Key, from Ex 39:29 to Lev. 13:25
SKIP 1014 letters to find Key encoded.

Key

- 'ter(ror)atak'
- → C(o)p(e)n-
- → -h(a)g(e)n
- → Den-
- → -mark
- → tribe,staff,ferule,clan,rod , February
- → YEARS 2019-2020=HC 5780,HC 5780=AD 2019-2020,AD 2019-2020=HC 5780

'ter(ror)atak', C(o)p(e)n-h(a)g(e)n, Den-mark, Shvat (February), HC5780 (2019-20).
Hebrew spelling of *Shvat* is 'Shbt.' For the correct year, see Appendix on how our
Gregorian Calendar needs adjusting by adding 4 to 9 years.

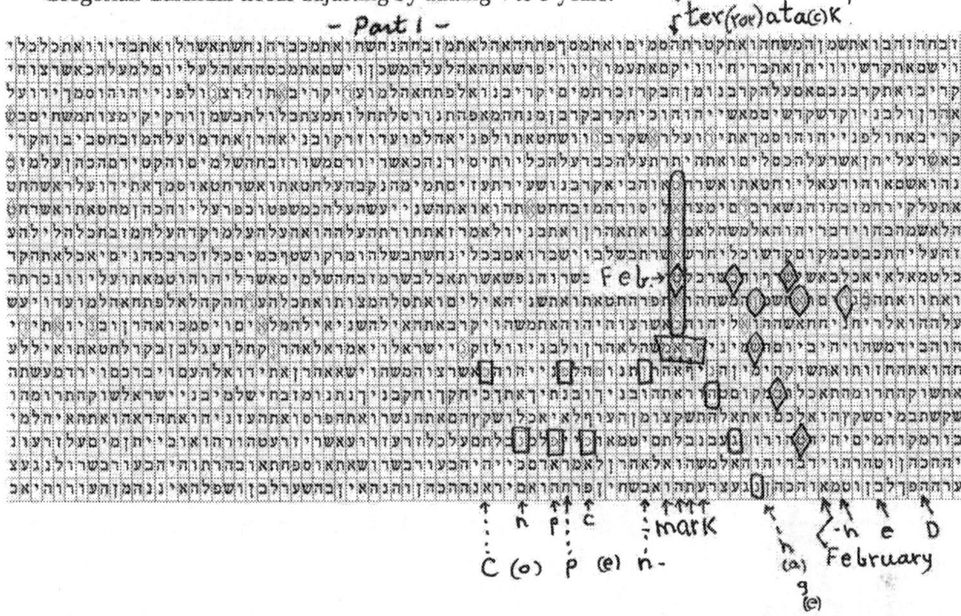

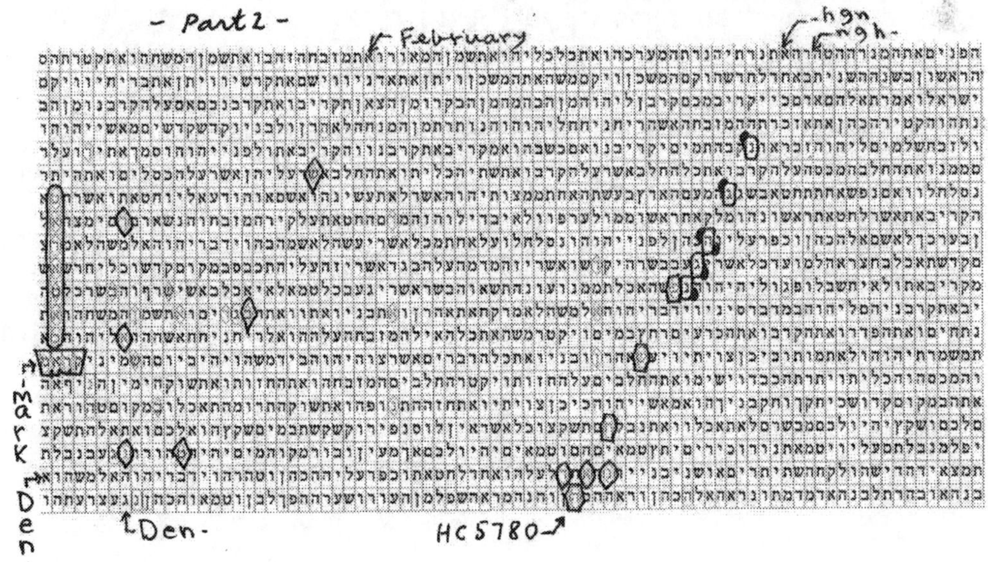

— Part 1 —

'ter(ror)ata(c)k'

Feb.→

↑ C (o)   P   (e) n-   ↑↑↑↑ mark   -h e D
      h   p   c   February
                                      (a)
                                      g(e)

— Part 2 —

↳ February   -hgn
                   ngh↴

-mark   Den-

↳Den-   HC5780↗

Fig. 27

Key

Tra(i)nCrash	טרע נכראש
	לעכ
Lac	מא גע
	נח ים
Mega-	קבב
	רכר
-ntic	םמא
Q(ue)b(e)c	
Can-	
-ada	

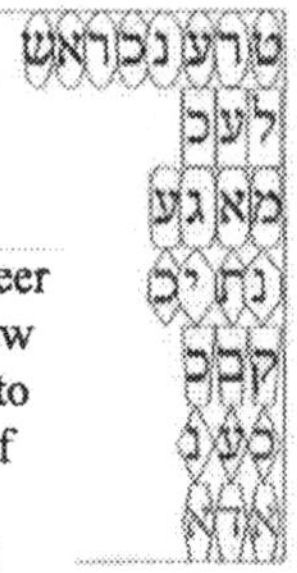

Fatal Train Crashes – This deadly train crash and oil spill (engineer walked away on a break, leaving the train un-manned, and somehow the brakes failed, allowing the oil-carrying train to roll *downhill* into the town's center, crashing and exploding) happened in the town of Lac Megantic, Quebec, Canada on July 6, 2013.
The downtown was completely destroyed in fire, killing at least 15 people, with about 40 missing; names to be found later and searched.

TrainCrash, Lac, Mega-ntic; Q(ue)b(e)c, Can-ada.

← Part B (next p.)

– Part A –   Tra(i)nCrash

n-ada →
-ada →
Lac →
-ada →

↳ Q(ue) b-(e) c

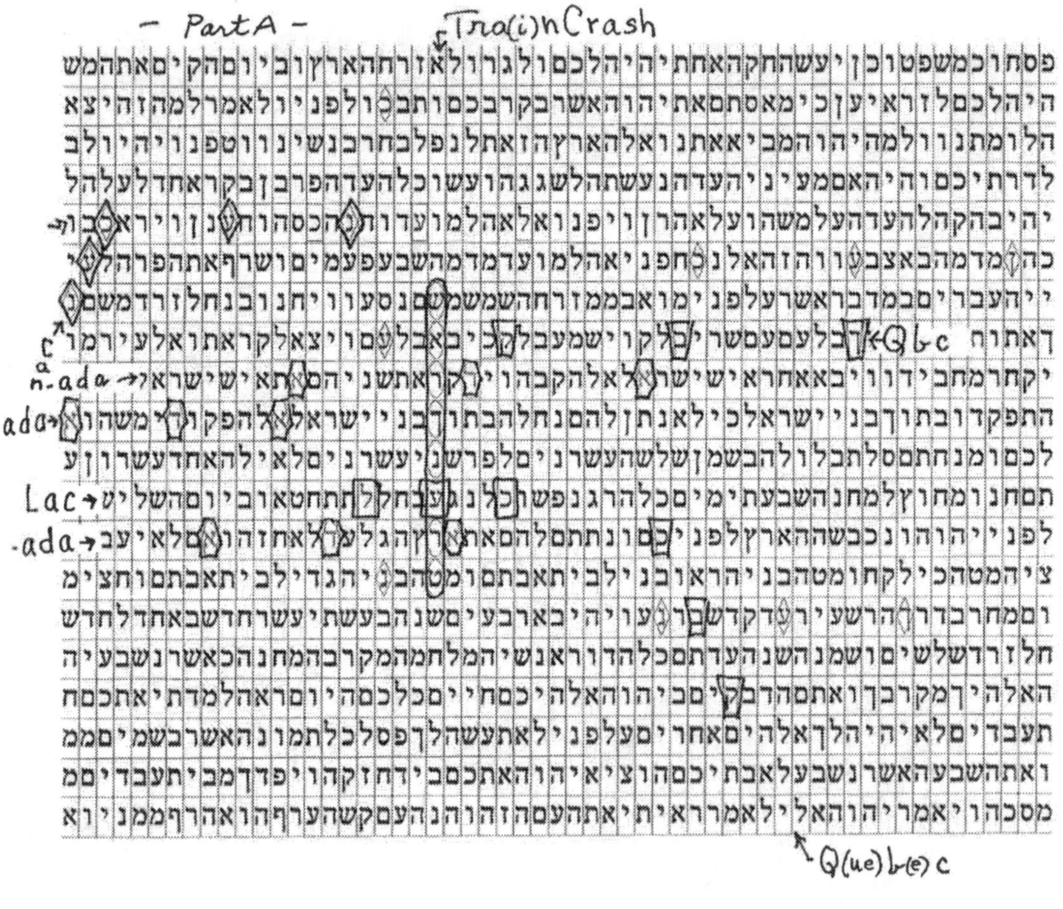

Fig. 28

Key

Tra(i)nCrash
Lac
Mega-
-ntic
Q(ue)b(e)c
Can-
Ada-

— Part B —

Note how town's name is encoded so close together in top center, with a shared -a- on row 2. Don't try such encoding of a large text at home, you'll hurt yourself. J.Satinover, MD, in his book *Breaking the Bible Code* (see References) cites NSA researchers who have concluded that humans today are not capable of such encoding of such a large text to such an extensive degree.

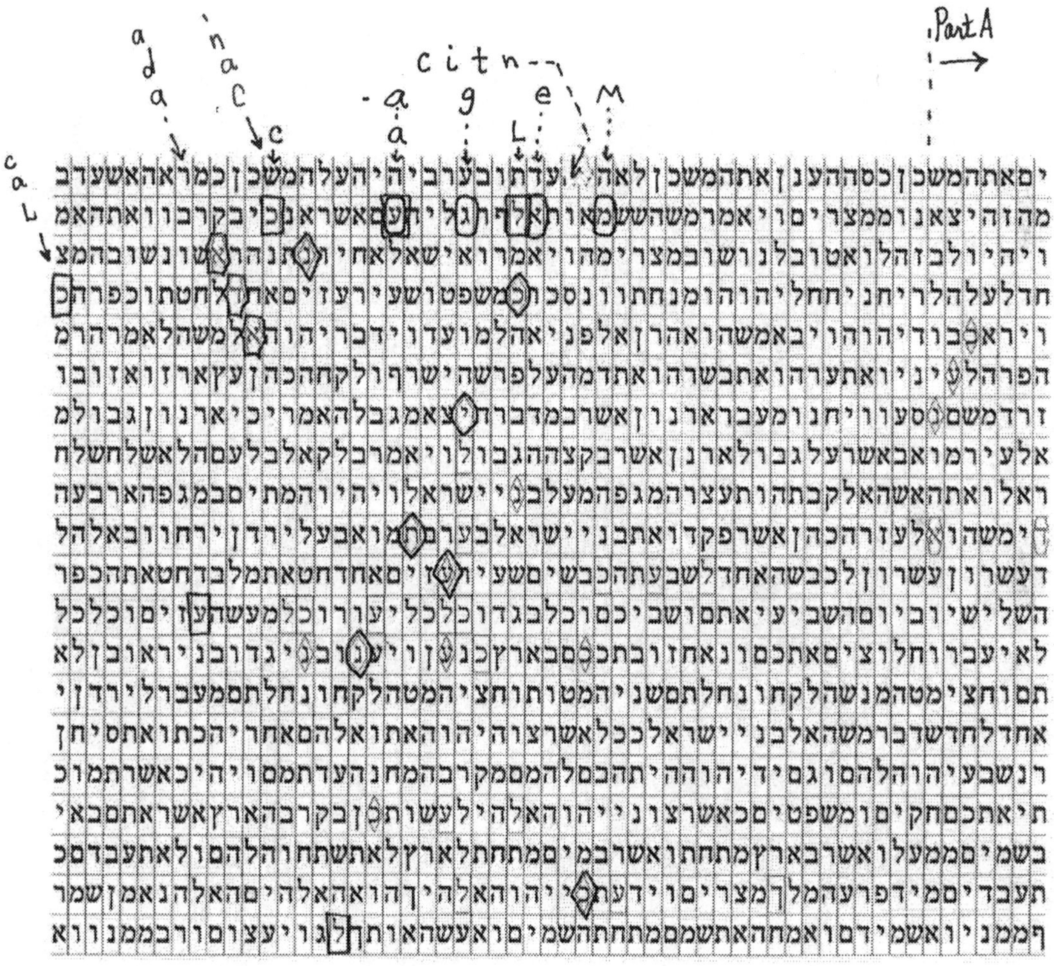

Part A →

Fig. 29

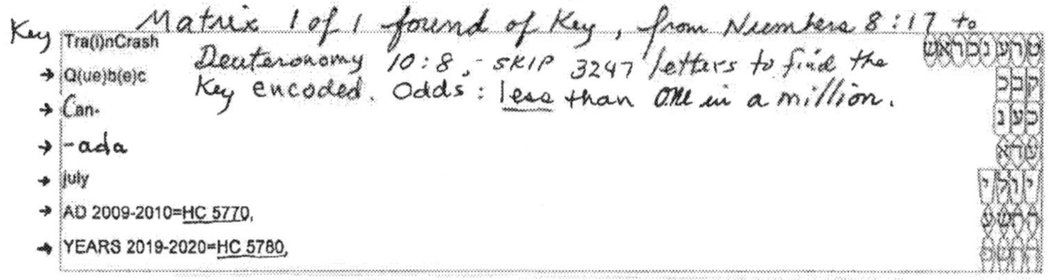

Matrix 1 of 1 found of Key, from Numbers 8:17 to Deuteronomy 10:8, - SKIP 3247 letters to find the Key encoded. Odds: less than One in a million.

Key:
- Tra(i)nCrash
- → Q(ue)b(e)c
- → Can-
- → -ada
- → july
- → AD 2009-2010=HC 5770,
- → YEARS 2019-2020=HC 5780,

TrainCrash, Quebec, July, HC5770 (2009-10), HC5780 (2019020).
The Key is transliterated, i.e., letter-for-letter sounds equivalent in English and Hebrew. For the Years, see Appendix on How Our Gregorian Calendar Needs Adjusting.

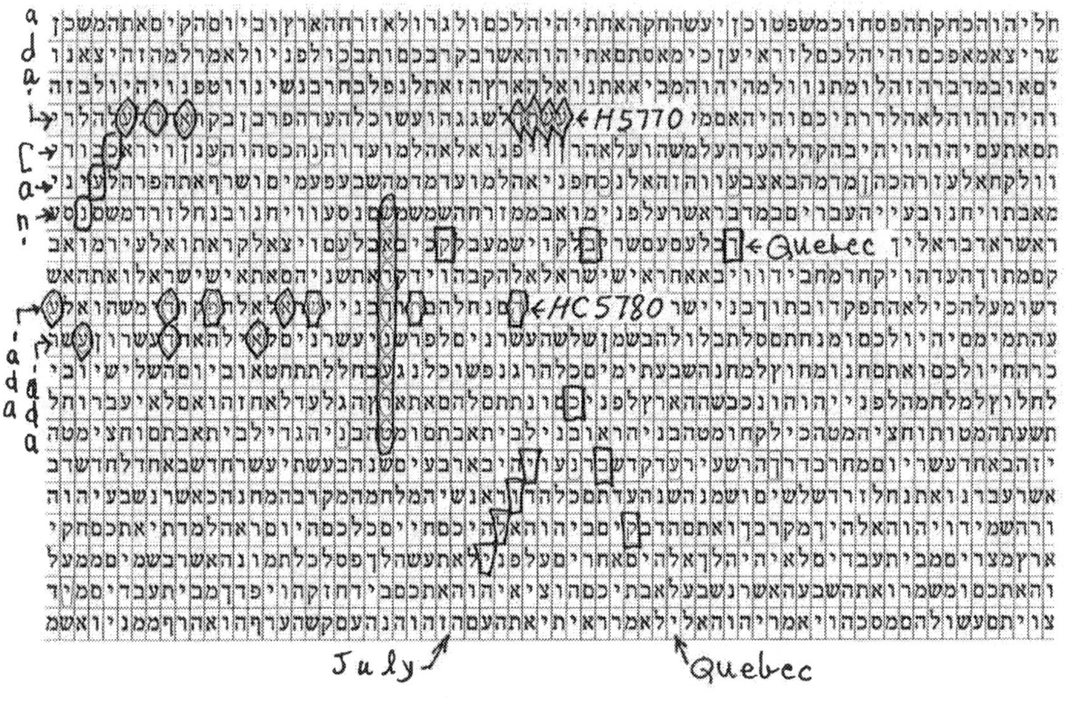

Just to left of this screen print are 3 more 'Can-' and a 'July.'
4 more 'Can-' could be labeled here, but note in upper left how the 2 parts touch each other. 'Quebec' (only 3 letters in Hebrew, is from the *Bible Codes Plus* program's Lexicon.

Fig. 30

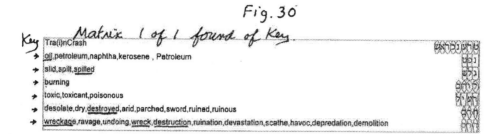

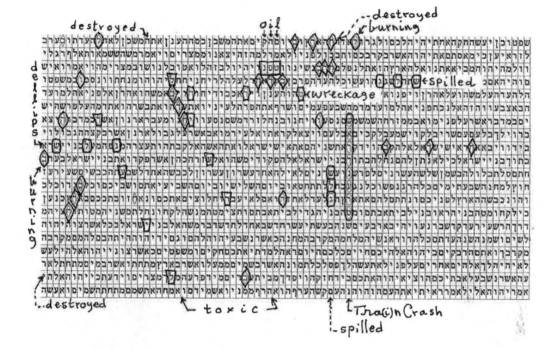

**TrainCrash, oil, spilled, burning, toxic, destroyed, wreckage/
destrĘuction.**

To left are 3 more 'destroyed.' 'Death' will be searched for when
names of all the victims are found and verified and searched for as
encoded in the Torah with the specifics of this horrible accident.

Fig. 31

SKIP 169 letters to find Key encoded. Odds of finding Key encoded in the Torah are less than one in a million.

Key
→ 'winOscar'
→ 'best'
→ 'Holly-'
→ 'movi(e)'
→ wood, cask, barrel
→ 'Acad-'
→ '-emy'

'winOscar', 'best,' 'Holly-wood,' 'movie,' 'Acad-emy.'

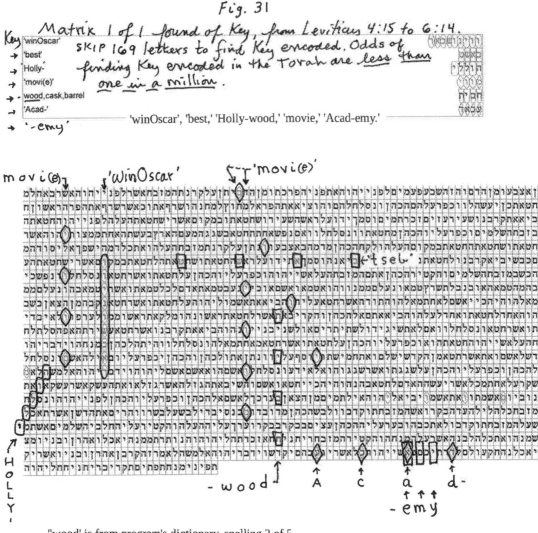

"wood' is from program's dictionary, spelling 3 of 5.
More '-emy' could be labeled here.
The letter *Aleph* is either -a- or -e-, so can be used correctly in both 'Acad-' and '-emy.'

Fig. 32

Matrix 1 of 1 found of Key, from Leviticus 4:15 to 6:14.

skip 169 letters to find Key encoded. Odds: less than 1 in a million against pure chance.

Key
- 'winOscar'
- 'best'
- YEARS 2019-2020=HC 5780,HC 5780=AD 2019-2020,AD 2019-2020=HC 5780
- 'movi(e)'
- manager,intendant,administrator,master,executive,headmaster,curator,director
- subvention,gratuity,bonus,subsidy,allowance,grant,award
- director,stagemanager,producer

'winOscar', best, 'movi(e),' HC5780, director, award, director.

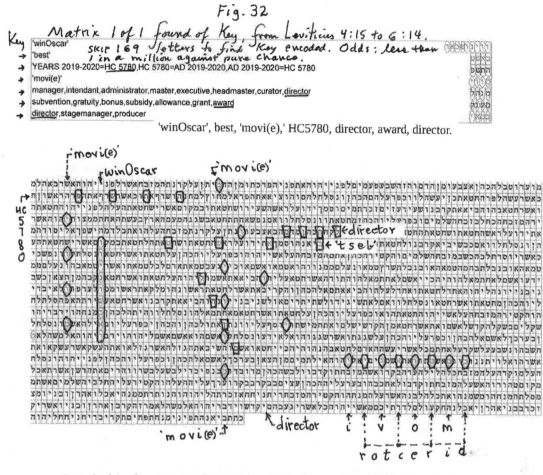

I was looking for winners in 2015. Hebrew Calendar year HC5780 is Gregorian Calendar year 2019-20 (from mid-Sept to mid-Sept); see Appendix for how it needs correction by adding 4 to 9 years.

To right, near column 1 (thus not printable) are 'award,' 3 more 'director' (trapezoid letter box shape), and another 'movie.'

Fig. 33

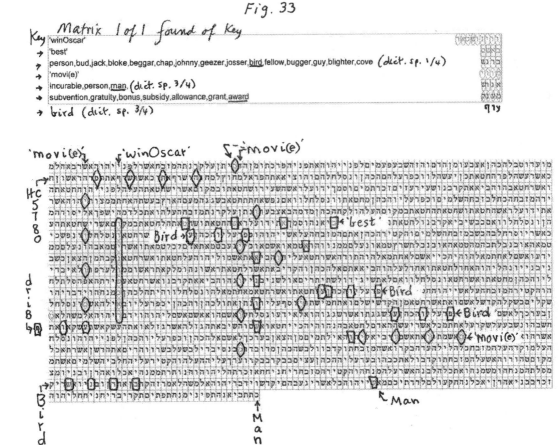

'winOscar', 'best,' award, 'movi(e),' Bird, Man, HC5780 (2019-20).

"Birdman" won best picture on Feb. 22, 2015 at the Oscars in Hollywood.
Note in center right, horizontal 'Bird' and diagonal 'Man' touch each other,
and that 'Man' is only 2 letters from horizontal 'best,' which is only 2 letters
from vertical 'movi(e).'
'Award' (dictionary spelling 7 of 7) is to far right, near first column (so is
unprintable), along with several more 'bird' (3 letters, dictionary sp. 3 of 4).
Note in center, vertical 'man' is only 1 letter away from horizontal 'bird'
(which touches transliterated vertical 'movi(e)' and is only 1 letter away
from horizontal transliterated 'best.'

Fig. 34

Matrix 1 of 1 found of Key, from Gen. 1:1 to Leviticus 8:22
SKIP 10,837 letters to find Key encoded.

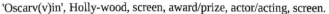

'Oscarv(v)in', Holly-wood, screen, award/prize, actor/acting, screen.

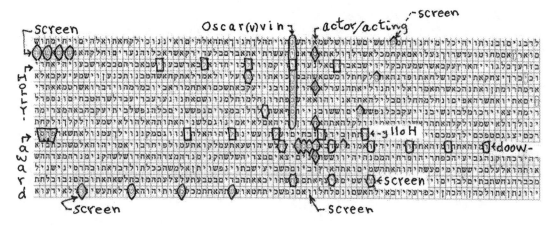

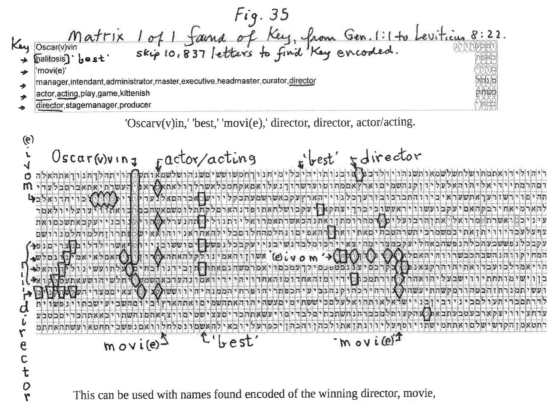

Fig. 35
Matrix 1 of 1 found of Key, from Gen.1:1 to Leviticus 8:22.
skip 10,837 letters to find Key encoded.

'Oscarv(v)in,' 'best,' 'movi(e),' director, director, actor/acting.

This can be used with names found encoded of the winning director, movie, and actor. To left of this screen print are 2 more 'movi(e)' and 1 more 'director' (first spelling on register above 1 of 2 in program's dictionary)
While the phonetic transliteration of 'best' from English in Hebrew means something, by coincidence, in Hebrew, it is the phonetic pronunciation that takes precedence in Bible Code research, so the English descriptor 'best' validly applies.

Fig. 36

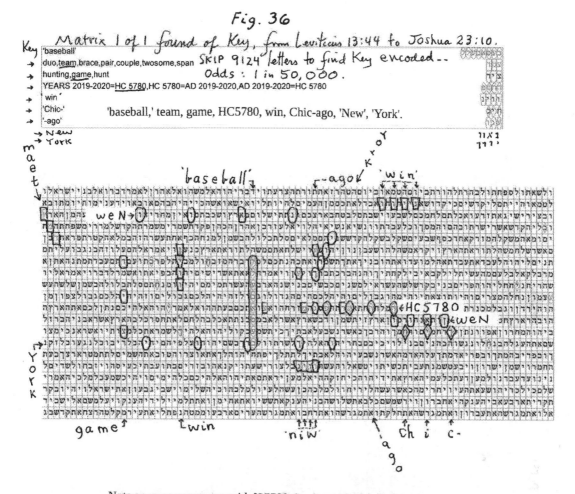

Matrix 1 of 1 found of Key, from Leviticus 13:44 to Joshua 23:10.
SKIP 9124 letters to find Key encoded--
Odds: 1 in 50,000.

'baseball'
duo,team,brace,pair,couple,twosome,span
hunting,game,hunt
YEARS 2019-2020=HC 5780,HC 5780=AD 2019-2020,AD 2019-2020=HC 5780
win
'Chic-'
'-ago'

'baseball,' team, game, HC5780, win, Chic-ago, 'New', 'York'.

Note on row near center, with HC780, is a 'team' (unlabeled), and the -g- of '-ago.' Perhaps an elegant prediction of pennant year in the 2019-2020 season, or thereabouts, per how the Gregorian Calendar needs correction of between 4 and 9 years, it being too low in its year count since the birth year of Jesus.

A copyrighted book is in progress by the author on the history of baseball as it is revealed encoded in the Torah.

Fig. 37

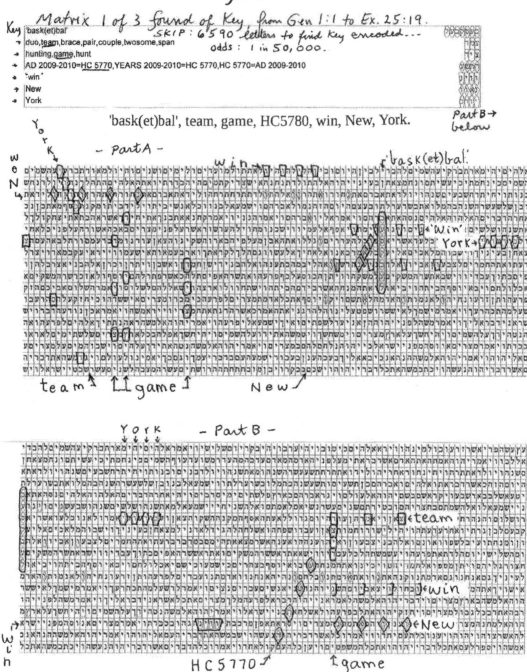

Note near top of the Key, 'New' and 'win' share a letter, and both touch the Key.

The author is working on a copyrighted book on how the history of basketball is found encoded in the Torah.

Fig. 38

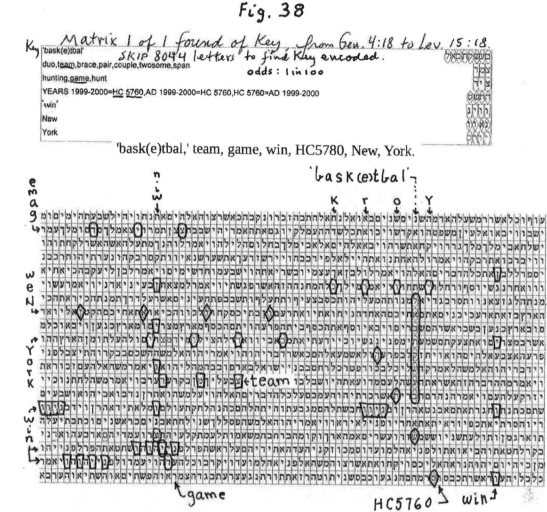

Matrix 1 of 1 found of Key, from Gen. 4:18 to Lev. 15:18
SKIP 8044 letters to find Key encoded.
odds: 1 in 100

Key
'bask(e)tbal'
duo, team, brace, pair, couple, twosome, span
hunting, game, hunt
YEARS 1999-2000=HC 5760, AD 1999-2000=HC 5760, HC 5760=AD 1999-2000
'win'
New
York

'bask(e)tbal,' team, game, win, HC5780, New, York.

Other cities and also team names show up as encoded, in the
copyrighted book of basketball history found Torah-encoded.
Also winners of games and divisions and championships.

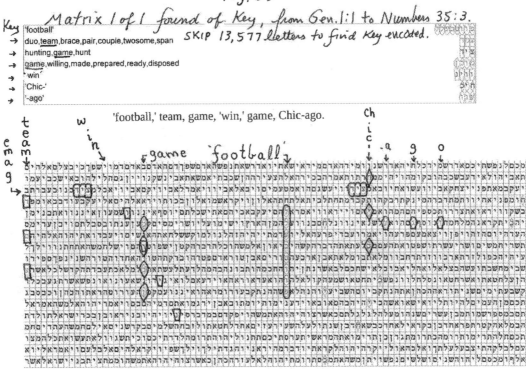

Fig. 39

Matrix 1 of 1 found of Key, from Gen. 1:1 to Numbers 35:3.
SKIP 13,577 letters to find Key encoded.

'football,' team, game, 'win,' game, Chic-ago.

Note left of Key how 'win' crosses 'game' and even shares a letter with it.
Further searches will reveal who Chicago played and when, and where they won.
Odds of finding this Key encoded just by pure chance are 1 in 5000.
A copyrighted book tracing the Torah-encoded history of football is in progress
by the author, including teams, leagues, names of players, games won and lost,
and championships won and in what years.

Fig. 40

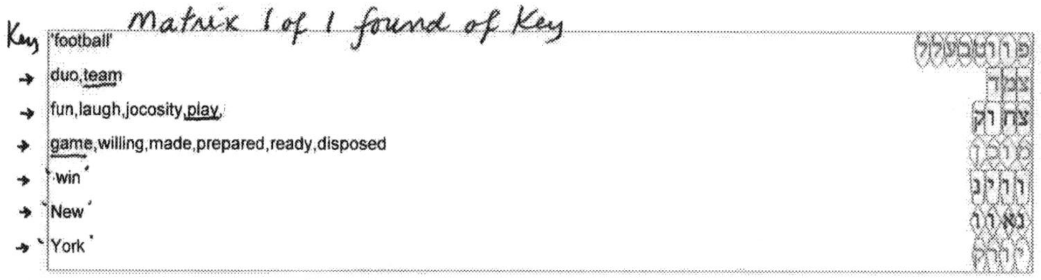

Matrix 1 of 1 found of Key
Key
'football'
duo,team
fun,laugh,jocosity,play,
game,willing,made,prepared,ready,disposed
'win'
'New'
'York'

'football,' game, play, team, win, 'New,' 'York.'

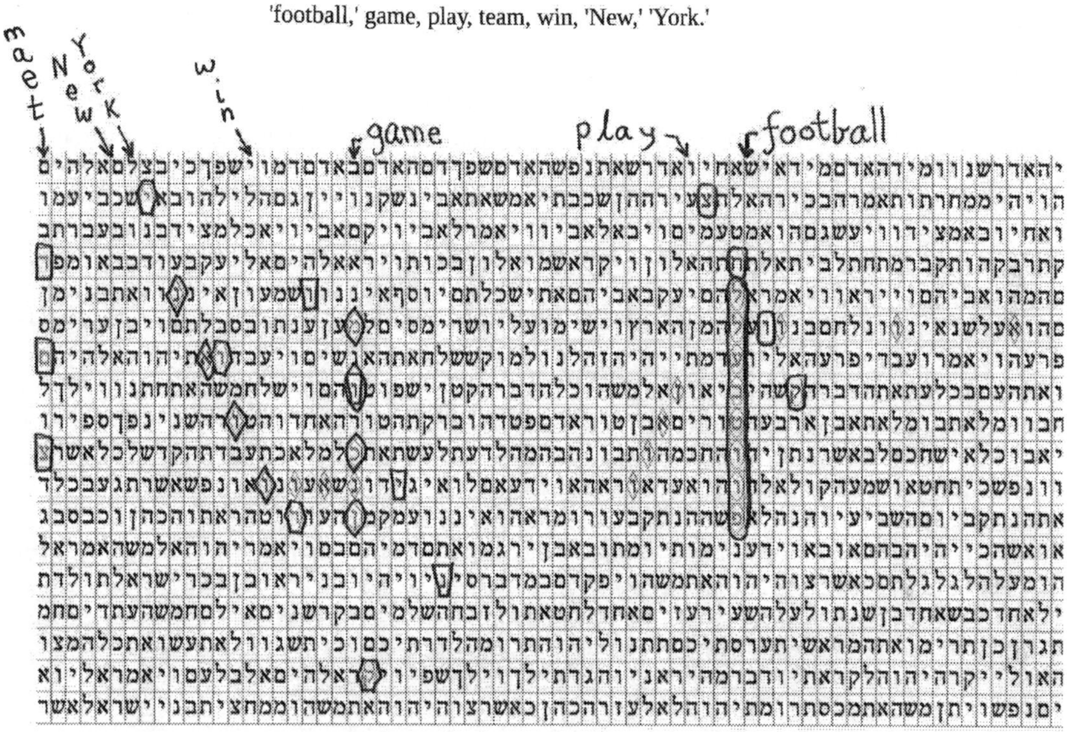

team
New
York
win
game
play
football

The verb form of 'play' is found encoded to the right of the Key and to right of this screen print. Another form of 'play' is shown here extremely closely related to 'football,' encoded diagonally, and even touches the top of the Key.

Fig. 41

Matrix 1 of 1 found of Key

'football,' game, team, play, 'win,' Den-ver.

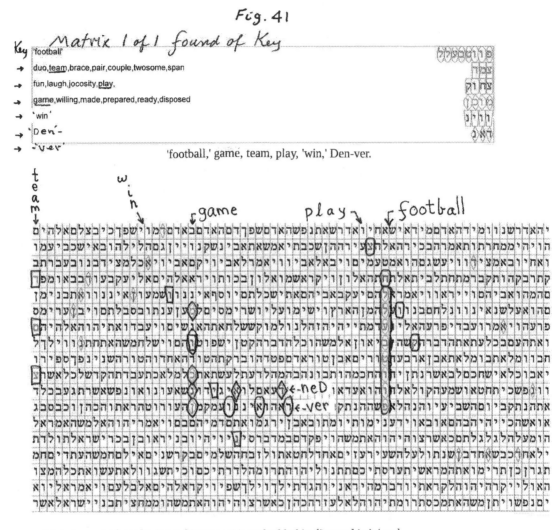

Note in center how horizontal 'Den-ver' is embedded in diagonal 'win' and
vertical 'game.' Other cities, and even teams and players' names will be shown
in the full-length copyrighted book manuscript currently being shopped
around to publishers.

Fig. 42

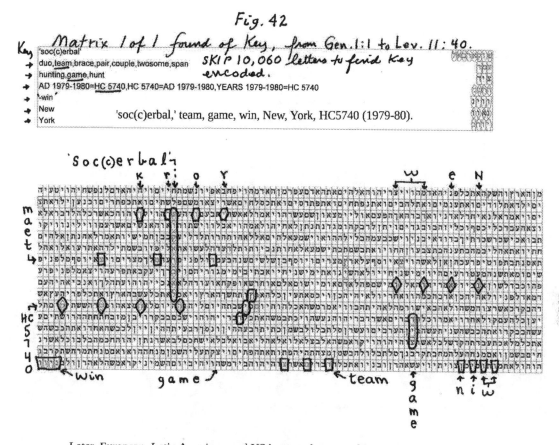

Matrix 1 of 1 found of Key, from Gen. 1:1 to Lev. 11:40.
SKIP 10,060 letters to find Key encoded.

Key

'soc(c)erbal'
→ duo,team,brace,pair,couple,twosome,span
→ hunting,game,hunt
→ AD 1979-1980=HC 5740,HC 5740=AD 1979-1980,YEARS 1979-1980=HC 5740
→ '-win'
→ New
→ York

'soc(c)erbal,' team, game, win, New, York, HC5740 (1979-80).

Later, European, Latin American, and USA teams, leagues, players, and championships found Torah-encoded will be included in the copyrighted full-length book manuscript being offered to publishers. In this Bible-Code investigative way, the whole history of 'soccer' (European football) can be presented in a dense and cogent way, with hardly any narrative needed in order to understand its development as a mature, organized sport.

Fig. 43

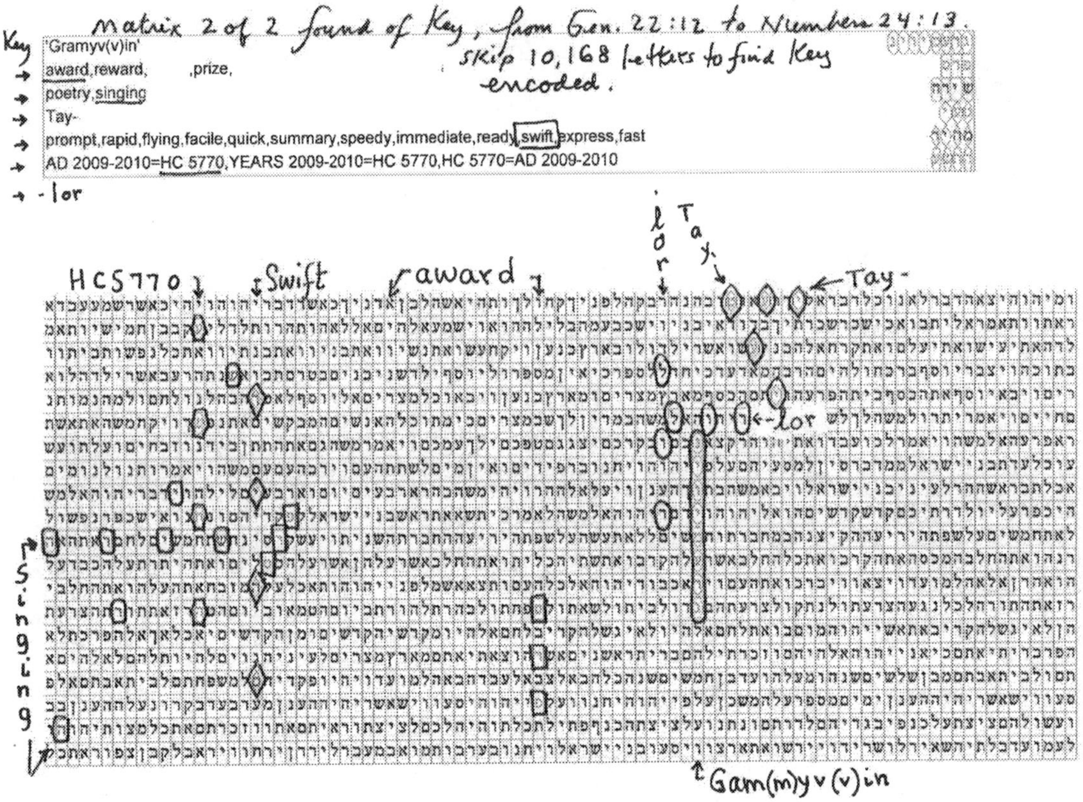

'Gram(m)yv(v)in,' award, singing, HC5770 (2009-10), Tay-lor, Swift.

Another HC5770 and a 'Swift' are to right of this screen print, about 22 columns.
More '-lor' could be labeled here. Other names and years are found encoded in
these 2 Matrices.
My whole copyrighted book of Grammy winners is in production; manuscript
being shopped around to publishers.

Fig. 44

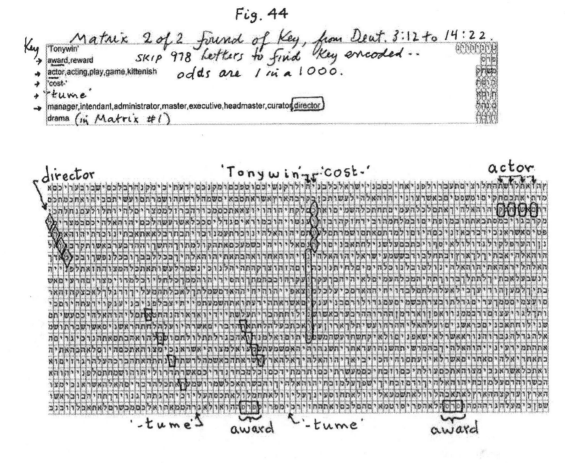

Matrix 2 of 2 found of Key, from Deut. 3:12 to 14:22.
SKIP 978 letters to find Key encoded..
odds are 1 in a 1000.

Key:
- Tonywin'
- award, reward
- actor, acting, play, game, kittenish
- 'cost-'
- 'tume'
- manager, intendant, administrator, master, executive, headmaster, curator, director
- drama (in Matrix #1)

'Tonywin,' award, actor, 'cost-ume,' director.

'drama' is in Matrix #1 (not shown in this book). Names and categories of the winners of this theater award, 'Tony,' are found encoded in these 2 Matrices — subject of a copyrighted book manuscript by the author, showing the whole history of who won it and in what category, and when.

Fig. 45

Matrix 4 of 5 found of Key, from Gen. 1:1 to Numbers 28:11
skip 13,543 letters to find Key encoded.

'boxing,' S[onny] Lis-ton, M.Ali, Fra-zer, For-eman.

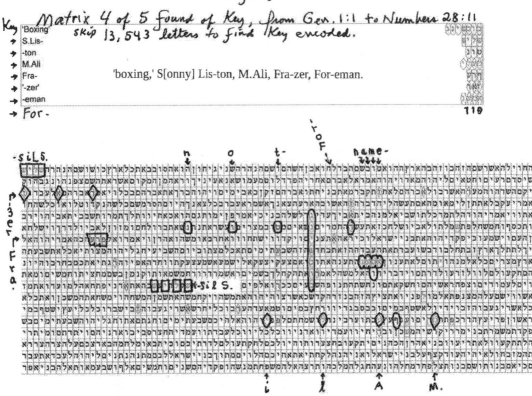

Since the -x- sound is made of 'k' and 's,' these 2 Hebrew letter-sounds are
used in the Key for the -x- spelling, phonetically.
Cassius Clay converted to Islam and changed his name to 'Muhammad Ali.'
The whole history of boxing can be revealed in these 5 Matrices containing
the Key 'boxing.' Interested publishers are alerted to author's manuscript.

Fig. 46

Matrix 5 of 5 found of Key, from Ex. 28:6 to Joshua 22:31.
skip 11, 295 letters to find Key encoded.

'boxing,' S.Lis-ton, M.Ali, Fra-zer, For-eman.

Key
'Boxing'
S.Lis-
-ton
M.Ali
Fra-
-zer'
-eman
For-

- Part 1 -

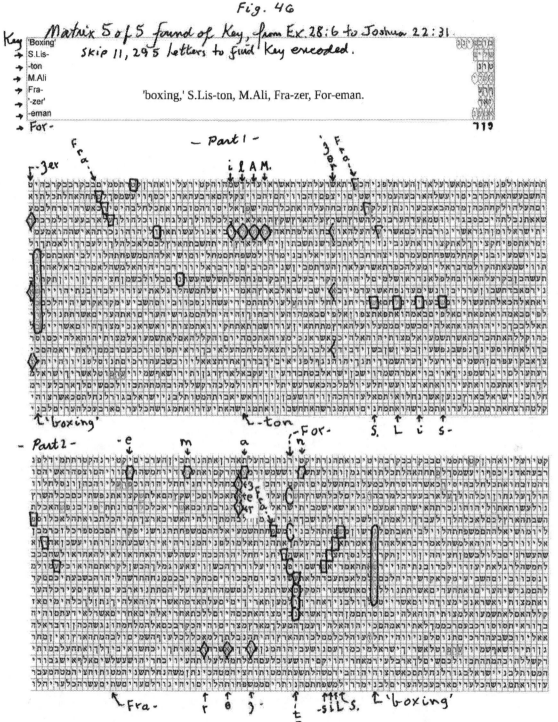

- Part 2 -

Fig. 47

Matrix 3 of 3 found of Key, from Exodus 2:21 to Leviticus 14:25.
skip 4,169 letters to find Key encoded.

Key
'bulfi(gh)ter'
→ 'tore-'
→ (generation, verticil, age, whorl) - '(a)dor'
→ 'mata-'
→ (generation, verticil, age, whorl) - 'dor'
→ (row, column, rank) TOR -
→ - 'ero'

Bullfighting –
'bulfi(gh)ter,' 'tore-(a)dor,' 'mata-dor,' 'tor-ero.'

'bulfiter'

'mata- -d o r'

-'ero' -rot

-'ero-rot

mata-

ero+ -rot -Tor

-Tor- -'ero

fiero rot ero t

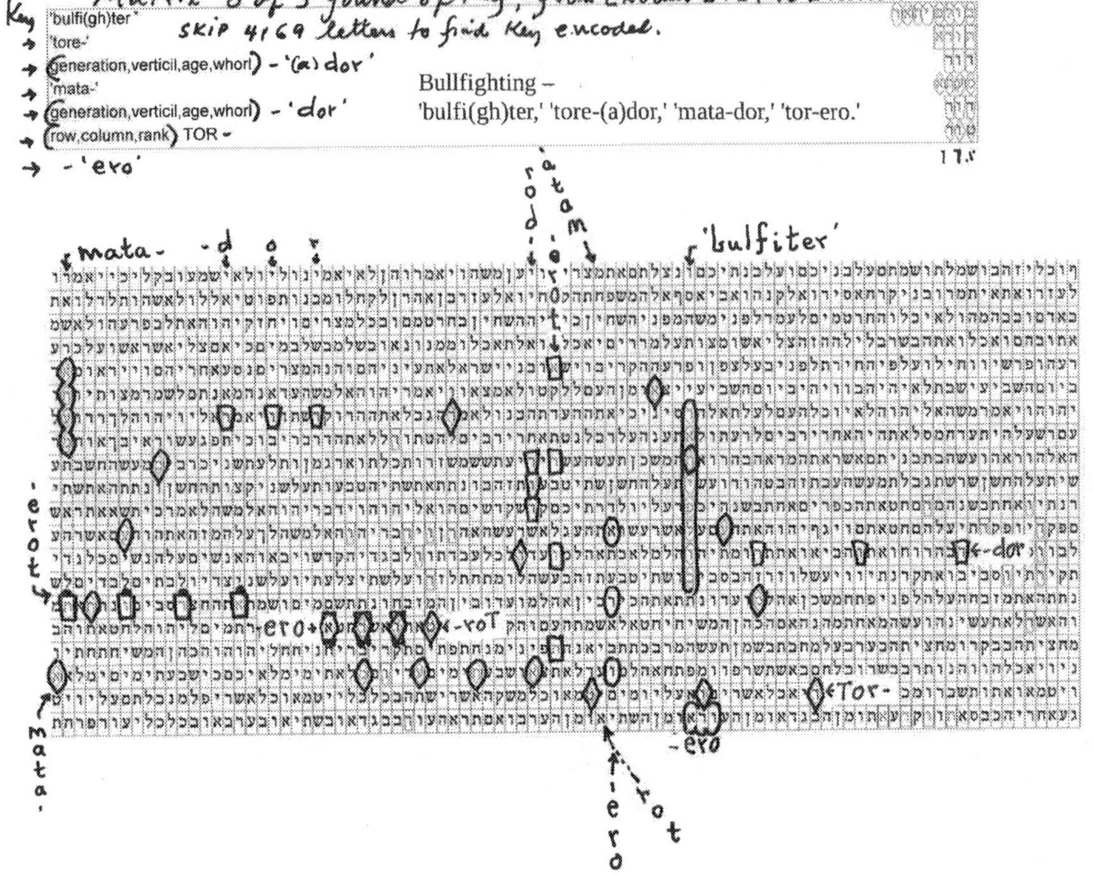

More parts are to the right of this screen print. Other aspects of this sport
are found encoded in this Matrix (and in the other 2 Torah Matrices with
this Key), as well as the names of the great bullfighters throughout history,
and the country in which they mainly fought, and the years of their careers.
Publishers are alerted about a developed, copyrighted manuscript available
for consideration from the author.

Fig. 48

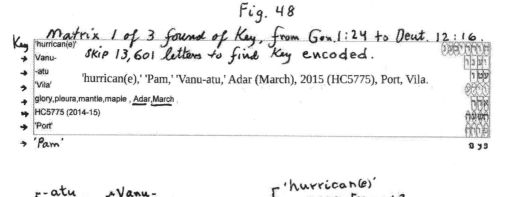

Matrix 1 of 3 found of Key, from Gen. 1:24 to Deut. 12:16.
Skip 13,601 letters to find Key encoded.

'hurrican(e),' 'Pam,' 'Vanu-atu,' Adar (March), 2015 (HC5775), Port, Vila.

Key
→ 'hurrican(e)'
→ Vanu-
→ -atu
→ 'Vila'
→ glory,pleura,mantle,maple , Adar,March
→ HC5775 (2014-15)
→ 'Port'
→ 'Pam'

A category 5 hurricane (called a 'cyclone' in the southern hemisphere) hit the
Pacific tropical island nation of Vanuatu on March 13-14, 2015, destroying
much of the capitol, Port Vila, and leaving 70 percent of the people homeless.
In this and other of the author's books a history of encoded hurricanes is being
documented and presented in black and white, along with 'tornadoes' also.

Fig. 49

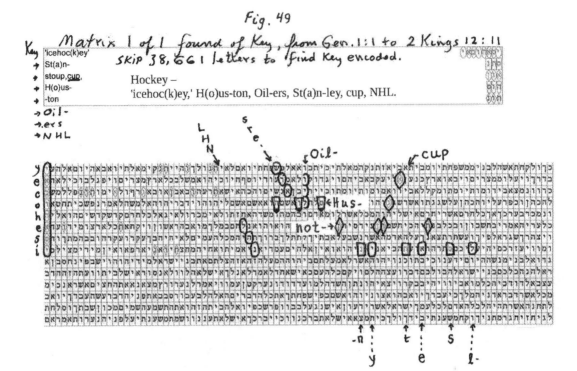

Matrix 1 of 1 found of Key, from Gen. 1:1 to 2 Kings 12:11
SKIP 38,661 letters to find Key encoded.

Hockey –
'icehoc(k)ey,' H(o)us-ton, Oil-ers, St(a)n-ley, cup, NHL.

NHL is the 'National Hockey League.'
-c- of 'ice' is phonetic -s-, so Hebrew letter *Samech* is used for this -s- sound.
The year the Houston Oilers won the Stanley Cup might be found encoded
here. Player's names and coaches could also be found encoded. Other teams
and members' names could also be found. The whole history of NHL hockey
could be presented in this one Torah Matrix.

Fig. 50

Matrix 3 of 3 found of Key, from Gen. 1:1 to 2 Samuel 24:9.
SKIP 27,629 letters to find Key encoded.

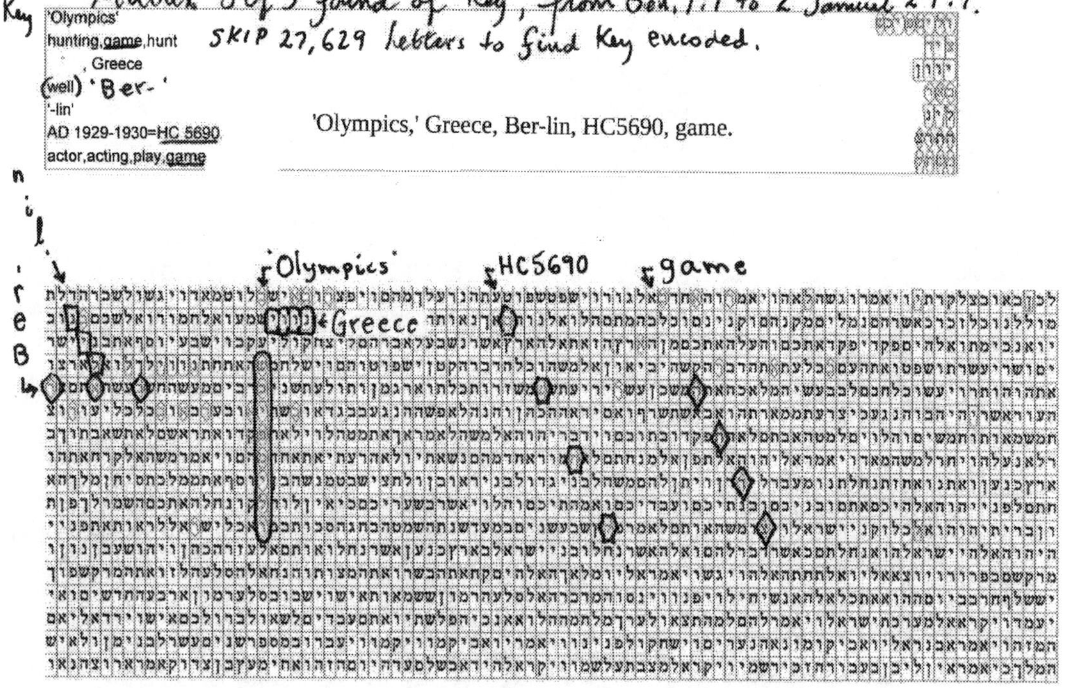

'Olympics,' Greece, Ber-lin, HC5690, game.

The Key is phonetic. The Olympics began in Greece as a set of sports games.
In 1946 the Berlin Olympics were held. The Hebrew Calendar year HC5690
lies within the calendar adjustment range needed to correct our Gregorian
Calendar (see Appendix).

The whole history of the Olympics could be found encoded, comprising a large
book which would include the encoded names of all participating countries,
location, both summer and winter, and all the sports, all the participants, and all
the winners of gold, silver, and bronze medals in all events.

Fig. 51

SKIP 764 letters to find Key encoded.
Odds: 1 in 500,000.

Key
- 'tenismach'
- Meraiah , MARIAH, MARIA, MERIA
- Shari-
- '-pova'
- 'Fr(e)nch'
- RUS
- YEARS 1999-2000
  (HC5760)

Tennis Match – 'tenismach,' Maria, 'Shari-pova,' 'RUS,' 'Fr(e)nch,' HC5760 (1999-2000). 'Rus' is old Russian for *Russia*. She is Russian, and has played in the French Open. Her other tournaments could be found encoded in these 2 Matrices. Other players and major tournaments could also be found, perhaps even much of the history of professional tennis. 'Wimbledon' and 'Australian' are found in both.

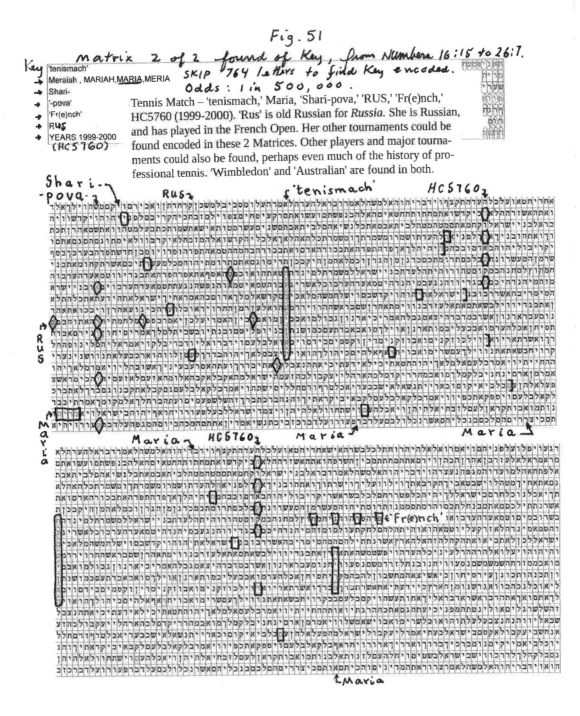

Part 2

Death's Torah Code

Below is most of Contents page of author's 2013 Author House book *Death's Bible Code* (each Part or chapter could be expanded into a full-size book – some have been already; and more associated names or events could be added):

Part 3

Predicting U.S. Presidents and World Leaders

Predicting Presidents
(and World Leaders)

On this site, 'Predicting Presidents.com,' a book by the author, me, Steve Canada, is offered and described in some detail. A separate volume, *'Predicting World Leaders,'* is also offered (see description and ordering information below).

I have found that **all** winners of U.S. presidential elections, from 1789 through 2008, are encoded in the Torah, **with** their opponents, some races encrypted with the correct year, and winners encoded by name as "**elected USA president**", and encoded with "**defeat**" of his opponent's name.

Future generations will need to use my method to verify any oracular potential of the Torah (the five Books of Moses, dictated to him by Yahweh about 3400 years ago) for use in future presidential elections. Its oracular, predictive power has already been demonstrated (such use of it is not biblically proscribed) by the Israelis, in politics (assassination of Prime Minister Itzak Rabin; warnings by Mossad not heeded), and in war (Israel town evacuated before it was attacked by Saddam Hussein's Scud missiles in the first Gulf War, 1990).

Can we develop a way to use the Torah as an Oracle, to be able to **predict** the outcome of a future U.S. presidential election? First we would need to know the main candidates running, that's why the timing of doing the research is so crucial, because the spelling of the names of those running needs to be entered on the Search list in the Bible Code computer program. Several such programs are available from Israel; I use 'Bible Codes Plus,' with my Dell laptop; no knowledge of Hebrew is required to do this Bible Code research – surprisingly only phonetic transliteration letter-by-letter is needed to get valid results in this 900-year old research tradition, discovered originally by rabbis that long ago.

I detected two distinguishing features in the search results that can be used to tell the winner from the loser. This is fully described, articulated, explained and **illustrated** in the book available on this site; see end of this Introduction for book's specifics and ordering details. In an attempt to use the Torah as an Oracle (not biblically prohibited), differentiating factors in search results were discovered that can be used to tell who would win any particular election. This research took exhaustive processing of **all** U.S. presidential elections held up to the present (April 2009), from 1789 to November 4, 2008, in order to confirm such distinguishing features found in consistent search results that would qualify as potentially predictive.

65

Not surprisingly perhaps, Alaska Governor Sarah Palin formed, in Feb 2009, a 'political action committee,' 'SarahPAC.' It is amazing to see how thoroughly and deep her whole political career in encoded in the Torah, down to the names of the towns in Alaska she served in various offices, and the years. For example: "Sarah Louise Heath Palin elected Alaska governor Juneau Nov 4, 2006." And: "Sarah Palin elected (to) Wasilla council Nov 4, 1996, and 2002, Alaska." Her middle name is 'Louise,' and her maiden name was 'Heath.'

As a condensed summary of the book's method and findings, search results are referred to below **without** the illustration of the encoded matrices of the Torah's Hebrew text. The 'Key' name is searched for at the maximum allowed skip (in order to get the most number of results, if any), which is automatically calculated by the program, depending on the length of the Key word in relation to the length of the whole Torah, which is 304,805 letters long. At the same time up to 6 other words or numbers (Hebrew uses letters for numbers) can be searched for; these 'other' terms are called 'Alternates;' they are either found encoded with the 'Key' or not, in the same matrix with the Key.

The 'Key' word, if found encoded, stands vertical in the Hebrew text, with all letters touching. The spelling order is either top to bottom or bottom to top – both equally valid as search results in Bible Code research tradition (see Satinover's 1998 book *Cracking the Bible Code*). The program searches the whole Torah (if that range is selected) forwards and backwards, starting at a skip of one letter, on up to whatever maximum skip is indicated by automatic calculation, or limited by the researcher.

Below are summarized the election results for much of the 19ᵗʰ century, as found encoded in the Torah:

In the 1824 U.S. presidential election John Quincy Adams ran against Andrew Jackson. Matrix #8 is printed in the book of the 30 'Key,' 'JAdams,' found encoded, showing "JAdams elected USA president [through] defeat." Matrix found from Genesis 18:22 to Leviticus 26:39; Key found at a skip of 8362 letters.

In 1828 they also ran against each other, but the results were reversed … "Jackson elected USA president [through] defeat." Matrix #2 is printed in the book of the 31 'Key,' 'Jackson,' found encoded, showing "Jackson elected USA president [through] defeat." The Key is found in this matrix at a skip of 16,837 letters, from Genesis 1:1 to Numbers 14:5.

In 1832 Jackson defeated Henry Clay. While Matrix #2 also applies to this election (see above for same finding), Matrix #30 of the 31 found shows "Jackson USA president, defeat Clay" – found at a skip of 17,289 letters, from Exodus 3:18 to 1 Samuel 20:37.

In 1836 Martin Van Buren ran against W.H. Harrison. Van Buren got 50.8% of the vote, versus 36.6% for Harrison (3 other candidates also ran). Of the 174 Matrices found for 'MVBuren,' #33 shows: "MVBuren elected USA president." Found at a skip of 11,736 letters from Genesis 1:1 to Numbers 9:15.

In 1840 they ran against each other again, with opposite election results. William Henry Harrison got 52.9% of the vote and Martin Van Buren got 46.8%. Matrix #2 printed in book shows: "Harrison president 5601, defeat Buren." '5601' Hebrew Calendar year encompasses mid-Sept 1840 to mid-Sept 1841, which includes the election month of November 1840. The Key, 'Harison,' is found at a skip of 12,086 letters, from Genesis 1:1 to Numbers 20:24.

In 1844 – "JKPolk elected USA president 5605 [1844], defeat Clay." James K. Polk (49.5%) defeated Henry Clay (48.1%). See book for Matrix print, skip, and Bible source in which this encoded result is found.

In 1848 – Zachary Taylor ran against Lewis Cass and Martin Van Buren. Search results show "Taylor elected 5609 [1848] USA president, defeat LCass." Here 'Cass' is spelled 'Kas' for phonetic equivalent. Matrix # 1 printed in book shows: "Taylor USA president 5609." Matrix #14, printed in book, shows: "Taylor elected USA president." Both shown of course with all the specifics of 'skip' and Bible sources in which these encoded results are found.

The 1852 election search results yield enumerated findings that can be summarized as: "Pierce elected 5613 [1852] USA president, defeat Scott." Franklin Pierce got 50.8% of the vote while Winfield Scott got 43.9%. The 'FPierce' matrix shows "FPierce elected USA president." The 'Pierce' matrix shows "Pierce elected USA president." Each are from different biblical sources and have different skips, as shown in the book.

In 1856 James Buchanan (45.3%) defeated John C. Fremont (33.1%) and Millard Fillmore (21.6%). Two matrices printed in book show: "Buchanan elected USA president" and "Buchanan USA president, defeat JCF." 'JCF are initials of John C. Fremont.

In 1864 Abraham Lincoln (55.1%) defeated George McClellan (44.9%). One matrix printed in book shows: "Lincoln USA president, defeat M[c]Cl[e]l[la]n." Another matrix shows: "Lincoln elected USA president."

In 1868 Ulysses S. Grant (52.7%) defeated Horatio Seymour (47.3%). Matrix printed in book shows: "Grant elected USA president, defeat S[e]ym[ou]r." This lack of vowel encoding conforms to ancient Hebrew in which there were no vowels as such. This matrix is so big it takes two screen prints, thus two pages in the book to include it all.

In 1872 Ulysses S. Grant (55.6%) defeated Horace Greeley (43.8%). Matrix printed in book shows: "UGrant elected president." While summary of all 102 matrices found with the Key 'Grant' would be, according to the tabulated enumeration of search results for all 6 Alternate terms: "Grant elected USA president, defeat Gr[ee]l[e]y."

In 1876 Rutherford B. Hayes (48%; 185 Electoral votes) defeated Samuel Tilden (51%; 184 Electoral votes). With 'Hayes' as the Key searched for, 4288 were found encoded; matrix #2 printed in book shows: "Hayes elected USA president." With 'RHayes' as the Key searched for, 199 were found encoded; summary of tabulated findings would be: "Rhayes elected USA president 5637 [1876], defeat T[i]ld[e]n."; matrix #3 is printed in book.

In 1880 James A. Garfield (48.3%) defeated Winfield S. Hancock (48.2%). Summary of tabulated findings of encoded terms searched in the Torah with 'G[a]rf[ie]ld' as the Key is: "Garfield elected USA president 5641 [1880], defeat H[a]nco[c]k." See print of matrix #10 in the book as sample.

In 1884 Grover Cleveland (48.9%) defeated James A. Blane (48.2%). Matrix #30 of 38 found of the Key, 'Clev[e]l[a]nd,' is shown in the book: "Clev[e]l[a]nd USA president 5645 [1884], defeat Blan[e]." Matrix #38 shows: "Cleveland USA president, defeat Blane." Matrix #11, not printed in the book, has: "Cleveland elected USA president, defeat Blane." Matrix #29, also not printed, but search results tabulated as recorded by the program, shows: "Cleveland elected USA president 5645 [1884], defeat Blane."

In 1888 Benjamin Harrison defeated Grover Cleveland. The summary of research findings as tabulated from program's search results is: "Harrison elected USA president 5649 [1888], defeat Cleveland." Print in book of matrix #4 of 6 found of Key shows: "Har[r]ison USA president."

In 1892 the results were reversed for these two same contestants. Tabulated search results show: "Cleveland elected USA president 5653 [1892], defeat H[a]r[ri]s[o]n." Print in book shows same result encoded in the Torah, from Numbers to Deuteronomy and a surprisingly small skip of only 1928 letters.

The election results were the same in 1896 as in 1900, with William McKinley defeating Willian Jennings Bryan. The 1900 results are encoded in the Torah thusly: "McKinley elected USA president 5661 [1900], defeat Bryan." Such findings also hold for the Key of 'WMcKinley' – matrix #2 of 3 found of such a Key, printed in the book, shows: "WM[c]Kinl[e]y USA president, defeat Bry[a]n."

The book connected with this site: *Volume One,* **"Predicting Presidents,"** 228 pages, 8.5"x11", $33.50 + $5.50 S&H; send check or money order to Steve Canada, 1123 N. Las Posas, Ridgecrest CA 93555. This Volume One includes all key samples of search results for **all** U.S. presidential elections that fully illustrate for demonstration purposes (it is assumed the reader or any other potential customer would never buy a book totaling tens of thousands of pages) the thesis of the project – answering the question: "Can the Torah be used as an Oracle to predict U.S. presidential election results?" Yes, they were predicted as found encoded in the Torah, but can we use the Torah as an *oracle* for the future? See *Postscript* (p.210), which explains why such an effort is not Biblically prohibited, while other types of 'foretelling' the future *are* specifically prohibited.

If so, then this will change our understanding of who we are vis-a-vis the composers and encryptors of the Torah (other avenues of the author's decades of research have answered that question; as a beginning, see his dozen interlinked websites, starting at www.CropCircleBooks.com. [site now defunct due to hosting service going out of business].

Volume Two, **"Predicting World Leaders,"** includes 16 countries other than the USA, some through decades of various rulers' names found encoded in the Torah, with their countries' names and year "elected.," and some with years of service. (208 pages, 8.5" x 11," $31.20 + $4.80 S&H). Fully illustrated, even with some original, hand-written research notes; if such presentation is offensive, please do not buy this book. Use above address -- ordering directly from the author is cheaper and much quicker than through any bookstore or book distributor. These two titles are not available in bookstores. Through distributors such as Ingram the price will be 20% higher, because they ask for a minimum 20% discount, and since I have been losing money on many such sales over the years, I thought it was about time I at least, as an independent self-publisher, begin to break even on such sales.

Part 4

Celebrities' Torah Code, Vol.1 – Their Deadly Diseases

Contents

Preface

Why are there so many deadly diseases? Why aren't we by this time, after about 30,000 years as a species, immune or completely resistant to many or most of them and their terminal effects? Is it an evolutionary struggle to destroy each other, pathogens, germs, bacteria, and viruses <u>us</u>, and we with our medicines and anti-disease research and disease-fighting regimens <u>them</u>?

How do we wipe-out disease, including cancers (the subject of Volume 2 of this 3-book series about what has afflicted celebrities and movie stars), and thus eradicate the attendant human pain and suffering? Will medical research eventually succeed in accomplishing this lofty goal?

The third and final Volume in this series will show celebrities and movie stars named in Torah matrices by categories of how they died in Accidents (plane and car crashes, etc.), Murders, Overdoses, and Suicides -- revealing as much as can be found encoded about the *where* and *when* and *how* and by *what* of those deaths.

What do these Bible Code, Torah Matrix search results show? These are not data-driven conclusions, but come from a function of language built on (as normal) an alphabet, an integral part of linguistic properties. How could it be otherwise, given we see the consistent patterns of Torah search results that reveal the mystery's functioning on the basis of phonetics in precise transliteration?

Statistical significance far beyond chance is revealed on at least two levels: (1) some of the odds of finding the Key (a searched-for word or phrase found encoded always vertical and with letters touching) encoded anywhere in the Torah (the Five Books of Moses, or sometimes the larger text) are less than one in a million; this is noted in the Matrix if such high odds are found, where the automatically calculated odds are found; (2) the odds of finding so many search results in the <u>same</u> Matrix are calculated by multiplying each of the odds together with each other, which results in a vanishing small chance.

So one of the questions I asked myself were: "Who died of what disease, and are their name and disease type found encoded together in the Torah Death Matrix?" There are dozens of types of deadly diseases. Millions of people die from them every year around the world. At one page per name found encoded with the disease type that killed them, it would take more pages per year than one researcher could produce, if all their names could be found, documented and verified.

The author is willing to hire and train a team of researchers if a publisher or research institute comes forward with a sufficient advance or grant adequate for the project.

Death rears its ugly head everywhere and at all times, in all sorts of situations and under many kinds of circumstances and from a myriad of reasons, affecting people in surprising ways, but eventually coming for everyone no matter their station in life. But why do we find their demises encoded in the Five Books of Moses? What is it about a sacred text of 304,805 Hebrew letters that enables it to hold the whole history of humankind, and encoded within it the specific circumstances under which particular people have died and are going to die?

Phonetics are the way to search for and evaluate the results here. Are the search results phonetically equivalent to what is searched for letter-by-letter in Hebrew? If so, then the result, what is found encoded, is valid as a Bible Code finding, in whatever spelling direction it is found. See Satinover, and Sherman on this point, in References.

"... a possible convergence between the Bible Code and quantum information processing ... something as astonishing and humbling as the Code – and the Torah to which it points. ..."
(Jeffrey Satinover, MD, author of *Cracking the Bible Code*; see References).

"Don't be afraid to see what you see." U.S. President Ronald Reagan

"Why shall we die before your eyes, ...?" Genesis 47:19

The Torah Code presents an anti-entropic technology (equal distance sequences of breath, i.e., sound of letters) that manifests as a means of moving beyond the limits of time ans space to connect with a universal truth articulated in recording our birth and our death, events connected to name-identity and located in a place and tracked by a calendar.

The mathematical probability of finding all these disease-related and personal biographically related specifics encoded close together in <u>one</u> Matrix, could be calculated by multiplying the probability of <u>each</u> found factor and name part by the other, resulting in a <u>very</u> unlikely chance that these encoded items would be found close together just by pure chance. See the 'Proximity' note in the Introduction. Such a finding reveals the <u>intentional</u> nature of the Torah-Bible Code, per Satinover, and also Sherman (see References).

I would describe a facet of my current book series as beginning on a meditation on the junction of Life and Death. Is the Torah, the Five Books of Moses, in addition to being a secretly encoded history of humanity, also an Ancient Book of the Dead, an Oracle of Mortality? We see encoded in it all the names of those who have died from whatever causes, be it war, holocaust, natural disaster such as earthquake, flood, tornado hurricane, tsunami or volcano, from terror attacks, or accidents such as car crashes, plane crashes, ship sinking, train crashes, or from diseases, cancers, murders, overdoses, suicides – their names are all are found secretly hidden in the Sacred Word of Yahweh, along with the causes of their deaths. Some are presented and shown graphically in this book; others are revealed in other titles by the author; see Book List.

I hope it is obvious this book is not exhaustive – there are hundreds, if not thousands, more celebrities and movie stars who would be included in any attempt at compiling a complete list of those who have died, the causes of which would invariably be found Bible-encoded if only an attempt was made at such a comprehensive search. Contractual restrictions require a small book such as this to serve the purpose of introducing the potential of what could be found and presented if production and pecuniary limitations didn't apply.

In fact, each cause of death list (chapters) as shown here could be expanded with inclusion of more and more names throughout the history of celebrity in various fields of endeavor ... the length of which would comprise an extensive book for each cause of death. In other words, this book is of necessity only a sampling of what hopefully could be a series of longer books investigating this strange record of death preserved secretly encrypted in the Sacred Word of Yahweh we see in the Torah.

Some people might have a preconceived notion of how encoded names should look as found in the Torah's text (albeit shifted to find the Key encoded), and since what is revealed in the matrices does not conform to their idea of how found names should be configured, they discount out of hand what they see with their own eyes. They think it's some sort of trick or misleading manipulation or illegitimate way to discover names of people buried in the Word of Yahweh.

The method of discovery used here has so far not failed to reveal the name of anyone searched for in the Torah, as long as they have been searched for with an appropriate and relevant Key pertinent to them personally, that is, historically connected to that name. Sometimes the name itself can be found as the Key, and then other terms searched relevant to and descriptive of the event in question will be found encoded close to the Key in that Matrix.

Predictive analytics become problematic when and if we take seriously Yahweh's injunction about using certain means to try and predict the future; see biblical reference source at end of "Short Media Interview" near end of this book.

Temporal asymmetry is an unseen obstacle as we try to grasp the significance of finding such dense encodings in the Torah that seem to encompass and describe in detail all of human history, right up to today's headlines, and this in a text thousands of years old (about 3400 years; according to the Orthodox view it was dictated to Moses by Yahweh on Mt. Sinai).

Part 5

Celebrities' Torah Code, Vol.2
– Their Fatal Cancers

Contents

About the Book

Celebrities and movie stars, like everyone else, die from a variety of causes, including *diseases* (Vol.1 of this book) and *cancers* (Vol.2 of this book). When we ask if such causes of death are found encoded in the Torah along with the encoded names of who died from them, we find them **all** close together in **one** Torah Matrix (from Gen. 1:1 to 1 Samuel 10:17).

For those uninitiated into the Bible Code mystery this might sound outlandish and impossible, but viewing the many Torah Matrices in this book, labeled clearly in black and white as secretly encoded facts staring us in the face might give pause to even the biggest skeptic.

Volume 3 of this book will show the Torah-Bible Code Matrices of celebrities and movie stars' deaths by *accidents, murders, overdoses,* and *suicides* – their names found encoded in the Five Books of Moses, some with the year and location of their death; as another e-book through Author House, later in 2014.

Thousands of similar results have been found by the author, covering many sorts of historical events ranging from the names of victims of natural disasters (e.g., *Fukushima)*, ships sinking (e.g., *Titanic*), planes and trains and cars crashing (e.g. James Dean), assassinations worldwide over 4000 years (e.g., an Egyptian pharaoh, JFK, and John Lennon), Nazi Holocaust, mass shootings (Aurora, Columbine, Tucson, etc.), terror attacks (Benghazi, Boston Marathon, Fort Hood, 9/11), and war casualties (e.g., Vietnam, Gulf War, Iraq, Afghanistan).

Even though there are only about 50 or fewer personalities identified by name in each of these three volumes, and shown encoded with how and where they died, each Volume could be expanded to hold many thousands of names and pages, one name per page of Matrix revealing those Torah-held secrets hidden for about 3400 years, and revealed here to the world for the first time in recorded history.

Preface

"You are more than just a movie star."
"Being a movie star's only half of it, baby."
(Part of exchange between Peter Evans and Ava Gardner, in
Evans' 2013 book *Ava Gardner, The Secret Conversations*, p.59)

Why are there so many fatal cancers? Why aren't we by this time, after about 30,000 years as a species, immune or completely resistant to many or most of them and their terminal effects? Is it an evolutionary struggle to destroy each other, pathogens, germs, bacteria, and viruses <u>us</u>, and we with our medicines and anti-disease research and disease-fighting regimens <u>them</u>?

How do we wipe-out *disease* (the subject of Vol. 1), including *cancers* (the subject of Volume 2 of this 3-book series about what has afflicted celebrities and movie stars), and thus eradicate the attendant human pain and suffering? Will medical research eventually succeed in accomplishing this lofty goal?

The third and final Volume in this series will show celebrities and movie stars named in Torah matrices by categories of how they died in Accidents (plane and car crashes, etc.), Murders, Overdoses, and Suicides -- revealing as much as can be found encoded about the *where* and *when* and *how* and by *what* of those deaths.

What do these Bible Code, Torah Matrix search results show? These are not data-driven conclusions, but come from a function of language built on (as normal) an alphabet, an integral part of linguistic properties. How could it be otherwise, given we see the consistent patterns of Torah search results that reveal the mystery's functioning on the basis of phonetics in precise transliteration, at least when a Hebrew word searched for is not found encoded?

Statistical significance far beyond chance is revealed on at least two levels: (1) some of the odds of finding the Key (a searched-for word or phrase found encoded always vertical and with letters touching) encoded anywhere in the Torah (the Five Books of Moses, or sometimes the larger text) are less than one in a million; this is noted in the Matrix if such high odds are found, where the automatically calculated odds are found; (2) the odds of finding so many search results in the <u>same</u> Matrix are calculated by multiplying each of the odds together with each other, which results in a vanishing small chance.

So one of the questions I asked myself was: "Who died of what cancer, and are their name and cancer type found encoded together in the Torah Death Matrix?" There are about two dozen types of fatal cancers. Millions of people die from them every year around the world. At one page per name found encoded with the disease type that killed them, it would take more pages per year than one researcher could produce, if all their names could be found, documented and verified.

The author is willing to hire and train a team of researchers if a publisher or research institute comes forward with a sufficient advance or grant adequate for the project.

Death rears its ugly head everywhere and at all times, in all sorts of situations and under many kinds of circumstances and from a myriad of reasons, affecting people in surprising ways, but eventually coming for everyone no matter their station in life. But why do we find their demises encoded in the Five Books of Moses? What is it about a sacred text of 304,805 Hebrew letters that enables it to hold the whole history of humankind, and encoded within it the specific circumstances under which particular people have died and are going to die?

Phonetics are the way to search for and evaluate the results here, unless a Hebrew word is found encoded. Are the search results phonetically equivalent to what is searched for letter-by-letter in Hebrew? If so, then the result, what is found encoded, is valid as a Bible Code finding, in whatever spelling direction it is found. See Satinover, and Sherman on this point, in References.

"... a possible convergence between the Bible Code and quantum information processing ... something as astonishing and humbling as the Code – and the Torah to which it points. ..." (Jeffrey Satinover, MD, author of *Cracking the Bible Code*; see References).

"Don't be afraid to see what you see." U.S. President Ronald Reagan

The Torah Code presents an anti-entropic technology (equal distance sequences of breath, i.e., sound of letters) that manifests as a means of moving beyond the limits of time ans space to connect with a universal truth articulated in recording our birth and our death, events connected to name-identity and located in a place and tracked by a calendar.

The mathematical probability of finding all these disease-related and personal biographically related specifics encoded close together in <u>one</u> Matrix, could be calculated by multiplying the probability of <u>each</u> found factor and name part by the other, resulting in a <u>very</u> unlikely chance that these encoded items would be found close together just by pure chance. See the 'Proximity' note in the Introduction. Such a finding reveals the <u>intentional</u> nature of the Torah-Bible Code, per Satinover, and also Sherman (see References).

I would describe a facet of my current book series as beginning on a meditation on the junction of Life and Death. Is the Torah, the Five Books of Moses, in addition to being a secretly encoded history of humanity, also an Ancient Book of the Dead, an Oracle of Mortality? We see encoded in it all the names of those who have died from whatever causes, be it war, holocaust, natural disaster such as earthquake, flood, tornado hurricane, tsunami or volcano, from terror attacks, or accidents such as car crashes, plane crashes, ship sinking, train crashes, or from diseases, cancers, murders, overdoses, suicides – their names are all are found secretly hidden in the Sacred Word of Yahweh, along with the causes of their deaths. Some are presented and shown graphically in this book; others are revealed in other titles by the author; see Book List.

I hope it is obvious this book is not exhaustive – there are hundreds, if not thousands, more celebrities and movie stars who would be included in any attempt at compiling a complete list of those who have died, the causes of which would invariably be found Bible-encoded if only an attempt was made at such a comprehensive search. Contractual restrictions require a small book such as this to serve the purpose of introducing the potential of what could be found and presented if production and pecuniary limitations didn't apply.

In fact, each cause of death list (chapters) as shown here could be expanded with inclusion of more and more names throughout the history of celebrity in various fields of endeavor ... the length of which would comprise an extensive book for each cause of death. In other words, this book is of necessity only a sampling of what hopefully could be a series of longer books investigating this strange record of death preserved secretly encrypted in the Sacred Word of Yahweh we see in the Torah.

Some people might have a preconceived notion of how encoded names should look as found in the Torah's text (albeit shifted to find the Key encoded), and since what is revealed in the matrices does not conform to their idea of how found names should be configured, they discount out of hand what they see with their own eyes. They think it's some sort of trick or misleading manipulation or illegitimate way to discover names of people buried in the Word of Yahweh.

The method of discovery used here has so far not failed to reveal the name of anyone searched for in the Torah, as long as they have been searched for with an appropriate and relevant Key pertinent to them personally, that is, historically connected to that name. Sometimes the name itself can be found as the Key, and then other terms searched relevant to and descriptive of the event in question will be found encoded close to the Key in that Matrix.

Predictive analytics become problematic when and if we take seriously Yahweh's injunction about using certain means to try and predict the future; see biblical reference source at end of "Short Media (Self) Interview" near end of this book. I am glad to see that the Bible Code does not violate anything on that prohibited list, such as "divination, soothsayer, enchanter, witch, charmer, medium, wizard, or necromancer," as listed in Deuteronomy 18:10-14 (Hebrew Bible as used in the *Bible Codes Plus* computer program, the Torah text of which has been authenticated to be the same as the printed text of the Torah by the Koren Publishers of Jerusalem, Israel, 33 Herzog St., P.O. Box 4044, Jerusalem, Israel; see Koren's authentication dated December 4, 1990, on p.100 of guide book manual of March 2001 that comes with the computer program disc from Israel, from Computronic Corp., P.O. Box 102, Savyon 56530, Israel; www.biblecodesplus.com).

Temporal asymmetry is an unseen obstacle as we try to grasp the significance of finding such dense encodings in the Torah that seem to encompass and describe in detail all of human history, right up to today's headlines, and this in a text thousands of years old (about 3400 years; according to the Orthodox view it was dictated to Moses by Yahweh on Mt. Sinai).

Note on Hebrew text source used in the *Bible Codes Plus* computer program used to create the Matrices seen in this book: The differences between the Hebrew Bible ('Tanach') and the Old Testament are: the order of the books is not the same; the number of chapters in some books is not the same; the number of verses in some chapters is not the same; the English text of the Hebrew Bible is a translation of the Masoretic Hebrew text, while the translators of the Old Testament use generally Greek and Latin texts as their source. (See p.97 of the *Bible Codes Plus* manual that comes with the program containing the <u>original</u> Hebrew text).

Introduction

"My truth isn't necessarily your truth, honey, ..."
(Ava Gardner to Peter Evans, in Evans' book, 2013, p.74)

Celebrities and movie stars around the world die from different types of causes, among them <u>diseases</u> (the subject of Volume 1 of this 3 Volume series), <u>cancers</u> (Vol. 2, due out in April-May 2014), and <u>other</u> <u>causes</u> (Vol. 3: *accidents* [skiing, car crashes, plane crashes, fire, drowning], *murders, overdoses,* and *suicides* – all found Bible-encoded with their names; due in June 2014).

These are searched for, with the victims' names, using a Bible Code program, and surprisingly all are found encoded in the Torah. In Vol.1, deadly diseases of various specific kinds are found, along with the names of the celebrities and movie stars who died from them, all in the <u>same</u> Matrix (search result for the Key word, 'malignancy').

An attempt is made to put the Bible Code mystery in the context of *meaning*, in the book's Conclusion. Bible Code applications and methods are explained in the Preface, Introduction, and Addendum 1. An effort is made to propose a means to gain near immortality through DNA, mitochondrial transfer, as the '3rd parent' in gene replacement therapy for the Death Gene (that which controls the number of cell divisions involving telemeres at ends of chromosomes) from a certain mummy specimen in the British Museum; see Short Media Interview.

Many of these Death Matrix search results look like they are configured like a molecular fit of atoms, at least from a two-dimensional perspective of a 3-dimensional arrangement of valence bonds. What would a 3-dimensional model of them look like? See Appendix 2, "The Immortality Molecule" for a brief discussion.

Bible Code Program's dictionary search for "actor" (spellings 1 and 2 of 2) found none encoded here with this Key ('Malignancy' in Hebrew); also, 'acting' (spelling 1 of 1, which is same spelling as 'actor' spelling 2 of 2). The 'act' found encoded is spelling 3 of 9 in Program's dictionary, but means "statute, law, act," so is not appropriate for association here with the profession of acting. Perhaps 'thespian' search would have better results, or even transliterated phonetically.

Leonard Nimoy (age 82 in 2014; "Mr. Spock" on 'Star Trek') has lung disease (chronic obstructive), he informed Pers Morgan on CNN on Feb.10, 2014. He described himself as "a champion smoker."

He died in March, 2015. Later a Torah Code search of his death will be done and included in a future book.

David Brenner, American comedian, age 78, died on about March 15, 2014, of cancer. The radio and television reports did not specify what kind of terminal cancer caused his death, but might be reported later. When more on his cause of death is released, a Bible Code Matrix could be generated, and included in a future, expanded edition of this Volume.

Francis Crick, co-discoverer of the DNA molecule, died at age 88 in 2004, of colon cancer. In an expanded edition of this Volume a Bible Code Matrix could be included showing such a search result.

Also, 'swine flu,' as the virus H1N1 made a comeback in the 2013-14 season, killing several people in the U.S.. Later, a search for this disease and its victims in the Bible Code could be done, along with the Key word as 'malignancy' (as used in this volume), along with terms like 'swine, flu, virus, death,' and even the names of the victims who died, and maybe even the location (state and/or city) and date (at least the year of their death; with the proviso explained in Appendix 1 explaining how and why our calendar is so inaccurate).

Cancer, and List of Types

Cancer is a type of disease, a group of diseases characterized by the unrestrained growth of cells.

Physicians describe the extent or spread of a cancer using a process called staging. This aids in determining the most appropriate treatment and in assessing the prognosis. One system widely used for many types of cancer classifies cancers into four stages. In this system, stage 1 is early stage cancer with no involvement of lymph nodes and no spread of the cancer from its original site (metastases); stage IV is advanced cancer, with both lymph node involvement and distant metastases.

Cancer afflicts people of all ages and races, although about 77 percent of all cases are diag-nosed at ages 55 and above. Cancers vary greatly in cause, symptoms, response to treatment, and possibility of cure. The World Health Organization (WHO) estimated that there were 70 million cancer deaths worldwide in 2007. Deaths from cancers worldwide are projected to continue rising, with an estimated 12 million deaths in 2030. A healthy, non-smoking U.S. male has slightly less than a 1 in 2 lifetime risk of developing cancer; a female slightly less than 1 in 3.

"... cures for most killer diseases remain elusive. New cancer drugs that add only a few agonizing months of survival are laden with such severe side effects that many patients reject them altogether. Some cancer patients say no to these overpriced drugs to spare their families insolvency." (Life Extension Magazine, April 2014, p.13)

Bladder cancer: Smoking is the main risk factor for cancer of the urinary bladder; exposure to certain hazardous chemicals in the workplace also places people at risk. Warning signs include blood in the urine, pain during urination, and frequent urination. Early stage cancer can often be removed surgically. Additional treatment may include chemotherapy and radiation.

Breast cancer: This is the most common, though not the deadliest, cancer among women. Risk factors include advancing age, obesity, physical inactivity, alcohol use, hormone replacement therapy, a family history of breast cancer, and inherited susceptibility genes, particularly mutated BRCA1 or BRCA2 genes. Early detection of the tumor – typically by breast self-examination or, more effectively, by mammography – is critical in improving a person's survival rate. Treatment options include removal of the tumor (lumpectomy) or the entire breast (mastectomy), radiation, chemotherapy, and hormone therapy. [Pre-emptive removal of breasts with no symptoms is becoming more popular even among younger women, especially when genomics reveals a mutated gene or persistent family history. Also, 2% of breast cancer cases occur in men; men are able to breast-feed under certain circumstances, so have the required lactation structures in their breasts].

Cervical cancer: Sexually transmitted diseases (STDs), particularly genital warts, appear to be the major cause of cancer of the cervix (the lower opening of the uterus). Tobacco use and obesity also increase risk. The first noticeable symptom generally is abnormal bleeding or discharge from the vagina. Treatment may include surgical removal of the tumor, cryotherapy (freezing the cancerous cells), radiation, and chemotherapy. A vaccine introduced in 2006 protects against four human papilloma viruses (HPV) that are a major cause of genital warts and cervical cancer. The vaccine is recommended for girls and women before they become sexually active.

Colorectal cancer: Major factors that increase the risk of cancer of the rectum and colon include increasing age, inflammatory bowel disease, and familial history of colorectal cancer. Obesity, smoking, physical inactivity, alcohol consumption, and high-fat or low-fiber diets also increase risk. Symptoms include rectal bleeding, blood in the stool, and lower abdominal cramps. Because symptoms generally are not noticeable until the disease is advanced, people age 50 or more are advised to have periodic fecal occult blood tests and sigmoidoscopies or colonoscopies. Surgery is the most common treatment; chemotherapy and radiation may also be used.

Kidney cancer (not listed in source cited below): In the 1958 movie *The Long Hot Summer* (story by William Faulkner), Lee Remick's character says to her sister-in-law's character played by Joanne Woodward who's driving the convertible Lincoln with Ben Quick (Paul Newman, in the back seat, a hitchhiker they just picked up): "I'm getting a falling kidney jumpin' around this country road with you drivin'." See Matrix of "Malignancy ... Lee Remick ... kidney cancer."

Leukemia: This cancer affects bone marrow, the lymph system, and other tissues involved in forming white blood cells, resulting in excessive production of abnormal white blood cells. The cause is unknown, though exposure to viruses, radiation, and certain hazardous chemicals (benzene, for example) increase risk. Common symptoms include fatigue, fever, weight loss, swollen lymph nodes, a tendency to bleed, and pain in the bones and joints. Treatment options include chemotherapy, radiation, and bone marrow transplants.

Lung cancer: This is the leading cause of cancer deaths in the United States and worldwide. The great majority of these deaths could be prevented if people did not use tobacco. Initial symptoms often are not noticeable until the lung cancer has grown for 5 to 10 years; they include chronic coughing, shortness of breath, wheezing, and chest or shoulder pain. Treatment may include surgical excision of part or all of the affected lung, radiation, and chemotherapy.

Lymphoma: Cancers that develop in lymph tissue fall into two main categories: Hodgkin's disease and non-Hodgkin's lymphoma. Risk factors are unclear, though viruses or other infectious agents are believed to play a role in at least some cases. The fist noticeable symptoms of lymphoma usually is a swelling of lymph glands; fever, night sweats, itching, fatigue, and weight loss also are common symptoms. Treatment my involve chemotherapy, radiation, and in advanced stages, bone marrow transplants.

Melanoma: This is the deadliest type of skin cancer, and it may also occur in the eyes and other areas where melancytes (pigment-producing cells) are found. The major risk factors include cetain inherited characteristics (light-colored skin, blond or red hair, blue eyes), and exposure to natural and artificial light. More often, the first noticeable sign of melanoma is a mole that has one or more ABCD characteristics: Asymmetry, Border irregularity, Color variation, and Diameter greater than that of a pencil. If caught early, before it has penetrated deeper levels of the skin or spread to other parts of the body, melanoma is very treatable. Treatment options include surgical excision of the melanoma and, if the cancer has spread, chemotherapy, radiation, and immunotherapy.

Ovarian cancer: Major risk factors for cancer of the ovaries include advancing age, familial history of breast or ovarian cancer, and the use of fertility drugs and hormone replacement therapy. The most common symptom is an enlarged abdomen due to accumulation of fluid. Treatment options include surgical removal of the ovaries and other female sex organs, radiation, and chemotherapy.

Pancreatic cancer: Risk factors for cancer of the pancreas include tobacco use, advancing age, and obesity; pancreatitis, diabetes, and cirrhosis may also be factors. Symptoms usually are not noticeable until the disease has metastasized. Surgery, chemotherapy, and radiation may help ease pain and prolong survival.

Prostate cancer: Increasing age is a leading risk factor for cancer of the prostate gland. Other risk factors are a family history of the disease and ethnicity – African-American men have the world's highest incidence rates of prostrate cancer. Noticeable symptoms generally develop after the disease has advanced, and include difficulty urinating, pain during urination, and pain in the lower back, pelvis, or upper thighs. Treatment may include surgery, hormone therapy, chemotherapy, and radiation.

Uterine cancer: Cancer of the uterus (other than cervical cancer) typically begins in the lining, or endometrium. The major risk factor is exposure to the hormone estrogen; obesity, diabetes, and hypertension also increase risk. The first noticeable symptom generally is abnormal bleeding or discharge from the vagina. Treatment involves removal of the uterus and perhaps other female sex organs. If metastasis has occurred, radiation and chemotherapy may also be used.

(The cancer definition, types, symptoms, and treatments listed and described above are from *The New York Times Essential Guide to Knowledge*, 2011, St. Martin's Press, pages 430, 432, 433; see References)

Regarding lung cancer --

The winter 2013 magazine edition of "City News," the semi-annual magazine publication of the City of Hope, has an article on lung cancer, "Lung Lottery," pp.6-11, by Gary Hopkins. It says: "Research around genetics' role in lung cancer gains momentum. Much about the world's number one cancer killer remains an enigma. Everyone knows by now that lung cancer overwhelmingly targets smokers. But why do nine out of ten smokers never get the disease?

And why are female non-smokers, particularly Asian women, much more likely than male non-smokers to develop lung tumors? Scientists at City of Hope and elsewhere are increasingly looking to genetics and genomics for answers to the disease's mysteries. Scientists believe a mix of genetic and environmental factors causes lung cancer." (pp. 6-8)

"... quitting smoking is the best way to improve your odds of avoiding lung cancer. Smoking, which is linked to 80 to 90 percent of lung cancer deaths in the U.S., remains the most important environmental contributor to risk. But about 15 percent of lung cancers occur in patients who never smoked." (p.8)

Part 6

Celebrities' Torah Code, Vol.3 – Their Accidents, Murders, Overdoses, and Suicides

Celebrities and Movie Stars Death Bible Code, Vol. 3.
Their Deaths by Accidents, Murders, Overdoses, and Suicides.
Their Names and These Causes Are Found Torah-Encoded.

Steve Canada

Author of: (1) Bible-Encoded Crop Circle Gods (4 alien mysteries solved). (2) Foretold in Sacred Code (all of history encoded in the Torah). (3) Death's Bible Code (accidents, assassinations, holocaust, mass shootings, natural disasters, terror attacks, wars). (4) End of Days 2014-2018. (5) Heaven and Hell Are Full, Angels of All Religions Returning at End of Days, AD 2014-2018. (6) Celebrities and Movie Stars Death Bible Code, Vol. 1: Their Deadly Diseases; (7) Vol. 2: Their Fatal Cancers.

Celebrities and Movie Stars Death Bible Code, Vol. 3

"You must abide by what is written. ... Don't be afraid, ... there is a plan."
Mr. Jordan (James Mason) to Joe (Warren Beatty), in
"Heaven Can Wait," 1978 movie, with Julie Christy.

Contents

About the Book

Celebrities and movie stars, like everyone else, die from a variety of causes, including *diseases* (Vol.1 of this book) and *cancers* (Vol.2 of this book). When we ask if such causes of death are found encoded in the Torah along with the encoded names of who died from them, we find them **all** close together in **one** Torah Matrix (from Gen. 1:1 to 1 Samuel 10:17).

For those uninitiated into the Bible Code mystery this might sound outlandish and impossible, but viewing the many Torah Matrices in this book, labeled clearly in black and white as secretly encoded facts staring us in the face might give pause to even the biggest skeptic.

Volume 3 of this book shows the Torah-Bible Code Matrices of celebrities and movie stars' deaths by *accidents, murders, overdoses,* and *suicides* – their names found encoded in the larger Torah, some with the year and location of their death; as another e-book through Author House, in mid-2014.

Fatal accidents found encoded here range from skiing, car crash, drowning, plane crash, and fire. Their murders are also discovered hidden in the secretly encoded word of Yahweh, along with their troubling overdoses of various drugs, and their tragic suicides.

An attempt is made to put the Bible Code mystery in the context of "meaning,' in the author's Conclusion. Bible Code application and method are explained in the Preface, Introduction, and Addendum 1. In memoriam, two original poems by the author are shown in the Epilogue; his poems have appeared in literary journals in 5 countries over forty years.

Even though there are only about 50 or fewer personalities identified by name in each of these three volumes, and shown encoded with how and where they died, each Volume could be expanded to hold many thousands of names and pages, one name per page of Matrix revealing those Torah-held secrets hidden for about 3400 years, and revealed here to the world for the first time in recorded history.

Preface

"You are more than just a movie star."
"Being a movie star's only half of it, baby."
(Part of exchange between Peter Evans and Ava Gardner, in
Evans' 2013 book *Ava Gardner, The Secret Conversations*, p.59)

Why are there so many fatal diseases and cancers? Why aren't we by this time, after about 30,000 years as a species, immune or completely resistant to many or most of them and their terminal effects? Is it an evolutionary struggle to destroy each other, pathogens, germs, bacteria, and viruses <u>us</u>, and we with our medicines and anti-disease research and disease-fighting regimens <u>them</u>?

How do we wipe-out *disease* (the subject of Vol. 1), including *cancers* (the subject of Volume 2 of this 3-book series about what has afflicted celebrities and movie stars), and thus eradicate the attendant human pain and suffering? Will medical research eventually succeed in accomplishing this lofty goal?

The third and final Volume in this series will show celebrities and movie stars named in Torah matrices by categories of how they died in Accidents (plane and car crashes, etc.), Murders, Overdoses, and Suicides -- revealing as much as can be found encoded about the *where* and *when* and *how* and by *what* of those deaths.

What do these Bible Code, Torah Matrix search results show? These are not data-driven conclusions, but come from a function of language built on (as normal) an alphabet, an integral part of linguistic properties. How could it be otherwise, given we see the consistent patterns of Torah search results that reveal the mystery's functioning on the basis of phonetics in precise transliteration, at least when a Hebrew word searched for is not found encoded?

Statistical significance far beyond chance is revealed on at least two levels: (1) some of the odds of finding the Key (a searched-for word or phrase found encoded always vertical and with letters touching) encoded anywhere in the Torah (the Five Books of Moses, or sometimes the larger text) are less than one in a million; this is noted in the Matrix if such high odds are found, where the automatically calculated odds are found; (2) the odds of finding so many search results in the <u>same</u> Matrix are calculated by multiplying each of the odds together with each other, which results in a vanishing small chance.

So one of the questions I asked myself was: "Who died of what cancer, and are their name and cancer type found encoded together in the Torah Death Matrix?" There are about two dozen types of fatal cancers. Millions of people die from them every year around the world. At one page per name found encoded with the disease type that killed them, it would take more pages per year than one researcher could produce, if all their names could be found, documented and verified.

The author is willing to hire and train a team of researchers if a publisher or research institute comes forward with a sufficient advance or grant adequate for the project.

Death rears its ugly head everywhere and at all times, in all sorts of situations and under many kinds of circumstances and from a myriad of reasons, affecting people in surprising ways, but eventually coming for everyone no matter their station in life. But why do we find their demises encoded in the Five Books of Moses? What is it about a sacred text of 304,805 Hebrew letters that enables it to hold the whole history of humankind, and encoded within it the specific circumstances under which particular people have died and are going to die?

Phonetics are the way to search for and evaluate the results here, unless a Hebrew word is found encoded. Are the search results phonetically equivalent to what is searched for letter-by-letter in Hebrew? If so, then the result, what is found encoded, is valid as a Bible Code finding, in whatever spelling direction it is found. See Satinover, and Sherman on this point, in References.

"... a possible convergence between the Bible Code and quantum information processing ... something as astonishing and humbling as the Code – and the Torah to which it points. ..." (Jeffrey Satinover, MD, author of *Cracking the Bible Code*; see References).

"Don't be afraid to see what you see." U.S. President Ronald Reagan

George Aichele, in his 2011 book *The Control of Biblical Meaning: Canon as Semiotic Mechanism*, describes semiotic theory (sign and symbol signifiers) and ideology, and textual media and the technologies of language, among other issues and basic questions related to the control of denotations and connotations.

The Torah Code presents an anti-entropic technology (equal distance sequences of breath, i.e., sound of letters) that manifests as a means of moving beyond the limits of time and space to connect with a universal truth articulated in recording our birth and our death, events connected to name-identity and located in a place and tracked by a calendar.

The mathematical probability of finding all these disease-related and personal biographically related specifics encoded close together in one Matrix, could be calculated by multiplying the probability of each found factor and name part by the other, resulting in a very unlikely chance that these encoded items would be found close together just by pure chance. See the 'Proximity' note in the Introduction. Such a finding reveals the intentional nature of the Torah-Bible Code, per Satinover, and also Sherman (see References).

I would describe a facet of my current book series as beginning on a meditation on the junction of Life and Death. Is the Torah, the Five Books of Moses, in addition to being a secretly encoded history of humanity, also an Ancient Book of the Dead, an Oracle of Mortality? We see encoded in it all the names of those who have died from whatever causes, be it war, holocaust, natural disaster such as earthquake, flood, tornado hurricane, tsunami or volcano, from terror attacks, or accidents such as car crashes, plane crashes, ship sinking, train crashes, or from diseases, cancers, murders, overdoses, suicides – their names are all are found secretly hidden in the Sacred Word of Yahweh, along with the causes of their deaths. Some are presented and shown graphically in this book; others are revealed in other titles by the author; see Book List.

I hope it is obvious this book is not exhaustive – there are hundreds, if not thousands, more celebrities and movie stars who would be included in any attempt at compiling a complete list of those who have died, the causes of which would invariably be found Bible-encoded if only an attempt was made at such a comprehensive search. Contractual restrictions require a small book such as this to serve the purpose of introducing the potential of what could be found and presented if production and pecuniary limitations didn't apply.

In fact, each cause of death list (chapters) as shown here could be expanded with inclusion of more and more names throughout the history of celebrity in various fields of endeavor ... the length of which would comprise an extensive book for each cause of death. In other words, this book is of necessity only a sampling of what hopefully could be a series of longer books investigating this strange record of death preserved secretly encrypted in the Sacred Word of Yahweh we see in the Torah.

Some people might have a preconceived notion of how encoded names should look as found in the Torah's text (albeit shifted to find the Key encoded), and since what is revealed in the matrices does not conform to their idea of <u>how</u> found names <u>should</u> be configured, they discount out of hand what they see with their own eyes. They think it's some sort of trick or misleading manipulation or illegitimate way to discover names of people buried in the Word of Yahweh.

The method of discovery used here has so far not failed to reveal the name of anyone searched for in the Torah, as long as they have been searched for with an appropriate and relevant Key pertinent to them personally, that is, historically connected to that name. Sometimes the name itself can be found as the Key, and then other terms searched relevant to and descriptive of the event in question will be found encoded close to the Key in that Matrix.

Predictive analytics become problematic when and if we take seriously Yahweh's injunction about using certain means to try and predict the future; see biblical reference source at end of "Short Media (Self) Interview" near end of this book. I am glad to see that the Bible Code does not violate anything on that prohibited list, such as "divination, soothsayer, enchanter, witch, charmer, medium, wizard, or necromancer," as listed in Deuteronomy 18:10-14 (Hebrew Bible as used in the *Bible Codes Plus* computer program, the Torah text of which has been authenticated to be the same as the printed text of the Torah by the Koren Publishers of Jerusalem, Israel, 33 Herzog St., P.O. Box 4044, Jerusalem, Israel; see Koren's authentication dated December 4, 1990, on p.100 of guide book manual of March

2001 that comes with the computer program disc from Israel, from Computronic Corp., P.O. Box 102, Savyon 56530, Israel; www.biblecodesplus.com).

Temporal asymmetry is an unseen obstacle as we try to grasp the significance of finding such dense encodings in the Torah that seem to encompass and describe in detail all of human history, right up to today's headlines, and this in a text thousands of years old (about 3400 years; according to the Orthodox view it was dictated to Moses by Yahweh on Mt. Sinai).

Note on Hebrew text source used in the *Bible Codes Plus* computer program used to create the Matrices seen in this book: The differences between the Hebrew Bible ('Tanach') and the Old Testament are: the order of the books is not the same; the number of chapters in some books is not the same; the number of verses in some chapters is not the same; the English text of the Hebrew Bible is a translation of the Masoretic Hebrew text, while the translators of the Old Testament use generally Greek and Latin texts as their source. (See p.97 of the *Bible Codes Plus* manual that comes with the program containing the original Hebrew text).

These volumes expand as I keep reading and finding new, relevant, pertinent research to include. A book that should have been referenced, if not quoted in Volume 2 ("Their Fatal Cancers") of this 3 Volume series is Devra Davis' 2007 book *The Secret History of the War on Cancer* (NY: Basic Books). It "illuminates the underbelly of medical research." (Washington Post). "Davis diagnoses two of the most lethal diseases of modern society: secrecy and self-interest." ('O' Magazine). She is a member of the team awarded the Nobel Peace Prize of 2007, and is professor at the Univ. of Pittsburgh. Back cover of her book says in part: "Leaders of Big Tobacco, the construction industry, the chemical companies have underwritten research to treat cancer but have undermined and downplayed efforts to prevent the disease altogether. They have sabotaged major public health efforts to prevent cancer for private gain – at the expense of millions of lives. ... the tobacco industry wrote the playbook for manipulating science and manufacturing doubt – a strategy employed today by the boosters of asbestos and cell phones."

In that book, for "cell phone risks and studies" see pp.400-4007, 466-476, and 478. On p.410 she points out possible dangers from high voltage electric lines and their electro-magnetic fields as possible human carcinogen, and that the World Health Organization and the U.S. National Institute of Environmental Health Sciences have classified EMF as a possible human carcinogen.

"... existentialism of destruction. The whole story: blood, sensuality, and death."
(See Vian, 1997, p.36)

Introduction

"My truth isn't necessarily your truth, honey, ..."
(Ava Gardner to Peter Evans, in Evans' book, 2013, p.74)

Elizabeth Taylor died of congestive heart failure and a leaky valve, at age 79. She was born on Feb. 27, 1932, and died on March 23, 2011.

L'Wren Scott, 49, Mick Jagger's girlfriend (who he'd been dating for 13 years) was found dead on March 16 or 17, 2014 in her New York City apartment. Later reports might reveal how she died. First report said it was apparent suicide. If enough accurate is released and can be verified, a Bible Code Matrix of search results might be included in a future edition of this Volume. She was 6'3" (much taller that Mick) and owned her very expensive apartment outright.

Rudolph Valentino died in August 1926, of peritonitis (inflammation of the peritoneum, the smooth transparent serous membrane [with cells that secrete a thin watery fluid] that lines the abdominal cavity and is folded inward over the abdominal and pelvic viscera [plural of 'viscus,' and internal organ of the body, especially one located in the great cavity of the trunk proper; per Webster's]; see Robert Wagner, 2014, p.78.

Nancy Roberts, half-sister of the actress Julia Roberts, age 37, was found dead of a drug overdose on or about Feb.10, 2014. They had the same mother. When more information is released a Bible Code search might be done, if appropriate under the circumstances at the time, and results included in a later book, if judgment warrants, meaning that since Nancy was not a star or celebrity in her own right perhaps such a finding need not be published.

Celebrities and movie stars around the world die from different types of causes, among them diseases (the subject of Volume 1 of this 3 Volume series), cancers (Vol. 2), and other causes (Vol. 3: *accidents* [skiing, car crashes, plane crashes, fire, drowning], *murders, overdoses*, and *suicides* – all found Bible-encoded with their names; due out in late June 2014).

These are searched for, with the victims' names, using a Bible Code program, and surprisingly all are found encoded, in the Torah, the Hebrew Bible. In Vol.1, **deadly diseases** of various specific kinds are found, along with the names of the celebrities and movie stars who died from them, all in the same Matrix (search result for the Key word, "malignancy").

An attempt is made to put the Bible Code mystery in the context of *meaning*, in the book's Conclusion. Bible Code applications and method are explained in the Preface, Introduction, and Addendum 1. An effort is made to propose a means to gain near immortality through DNA, mitochondrial transfer, as the '3rd parent' in gene replacement therapy for the Death Gene (that which controls the number of cell divisions involving telomeres at ends of chromosomes) from a certain mummy specimen in the British Museum; see Short Media Interview.

In memorial for the departed, two original poems by the author are shown in the Epilogue; his poems have appeared in literary journals in 5 countries over 40 years and with at least one Nobel Prize winner for literature (Pablo Neruda, in *The Paris Review*).

 Chapters in some other books by the author are only representative samples from much larger, full-length Reports or whole Books on those subjects – available for ordering directly from the author – see Book List at end of this book. These are hand-made Reports and Books produced by the author; in these are shown the names of the dead from each circumstance as encoded in the Torah.

The Bible is encoded with many interesting names and phrases, some apparently predictive of historical events. These are discovered by counting any certain number of letters, that is, 'skipping' any chosen number of letters (ELS … Equidistant Letter Sequence) starting from anywhere in the original Hebrew text.

Code searchers usually restrict their work to the Torah, the first five books of the Bible; others use what Christians call the whole 'Old Testament.' It is recommended to read R. Edwin Sherman's 2004 book *Bible Code Bombshell*. He is a mathematician and eschews sensationalistic approaches to Bible Code discoveries. He is the founder of the 'Isaac Newton Bible Code Research Society,' located in southern Oregon; free membership and newsletter on website www.biblecodedigest.com.

Death's Bible Code: Names of the Dead Throughout History are found encoded in the Torah, the Five Books of Moses. From Ancient Egypt to Auschwitz to the Titanic to Sandy Hook Mass Shooting to Boston Marathon Bombing, all the dead's names are found encoded. Assassinations over 4000 years, casualties of wars, accidents, mass shootings, natural disasters, and terror attacks – their names are found secretly encoded in the sacred Word of Yahweh, *with* the name of the event in which they died.

"Why should we die before your eyes, …?"
(Genesis 47:19, in NLT, 1996, p.48, see References)

The embedded Torah information is clear, conspicuous and concise. The original Hebrew text seen in the chapters and sections in this book has not been changed even by *one* letter in about 3400 years, since the time Yahweh dictated it letter-by-letter to Moses on Mt. Sinai. I don't know precisely who composed and the dictated Torah, or how much care, effort, time, resources or editing went into its design or code architecture, but given what has been uncovered in the plain text just by counting between letters during the past 900 years of Bible Code study, the nature of the intelligence behind it is consistent with what is known elsewhere about the identity and abilities of Yahweh (see Sitchin in References).

Search for terms entered is done automatically by the Bible Code program (for example, *Bible Code Plus*, from Israel via USPS). Search is done forward, then backward, through the whole Torah (or within any range you specify); any spelling direction found is valid, be it horizontal, vertical or diagonal. No knowledge of any Hebrew is needed in order to do Bible Code research. Search terms can be entered using the program's dictionary or lexicon or 'dates' list, or entered phonetically using transliteration (letter-by-letter, sound for corresponding sound from English to Hebrew using the program's on-screen keyboard).

The first term the program will search for is the 'Key,' and if found encoded it will stand vertically with letters touching in correct spelling sequence, either top-to-bottom or the reverse. Any spelling direction of any term found encoded is a valid search result. For example, enter the Key as 'Titanic,' transliterated with Hebrew letter sounds, and only *one* such encoded word is found in the whole Torah, in *one* Matrix. Up to six terms can be searched for at the same time, along with the Key. All factors about that disastrous iceberg crash and sinking are found encoded in that *one* Matrix, along with *all* the names of those who died that fateful night (see Book List).

'Proximity' means the visual distance between the Key Code and any other code or word in the retrieved matrix. Bible Code research theory states that the closer the pairings are, i.e., the more compact the visual cluster effect, the greater their significance. Jeffrey Satinover, MD, in his book *Cracking the Bible Code*, says "there is a tendency for meaningfully related words to show the cluster effect, appearing in the array more closely together than unrelated words." (Quoted in manual that comes with the *Bible Codes Plus* computer disc, p.9).

The odds of the Key in any particular Matrix being found encoded by chance can go as low as one in a million or less as calculated automatically by the *Bible Code Plus* computer program (available directly from Israel). While the odds could be even lower than that, the program does not calculate below that. The encodement algorithm used by the Torah composers that allows such dense search results of the encoded found terms (whether in syllables or not) encoded so close to the Key (see 'Proximity' note elsewhere) and to each other, is a function of an unknown technology and encryption mathematics.

The essential sounds that comprise the encoded words are phonetically rendered coherent, readable and understandable through transliteration, finding the equivalent sound of the English letter in the appropriate, corresponding Hebrew letter that has the same sound as shown in the on-screen keyboard ... those strung together in correct spelling sequence, keeps the English sound of the word entered in the search function of the program; for example, 'Titanic' or 'Concordia.'

Many of these Death Matrix search results look like they are configured like a molecular fit of atoms, at least from a two-dimensional perspective of a 3-dimensional arrangement of valence bonds.

What would a 3-dimensional model of them look like? See Appendix 2, "The Immortality Molecule" for a brief discussion.

Bible Code Program's dictionary search for "actor" (spellings 1 and 2 of 2) found none encoded here with this Key ('Malignancy' in Hebrew); also, 'acting' (spelling 1 of 1, which is same spelling as 'actor' spelling 2 of 2). The 'act' found encoded is spelling 3 of 9 in Program's dictionary, but means "statute, law, act," so is not appropriate for association here with the profession of acting. Perhaps 'thespian' search would have better results, or even transliterated phonetically.

Leonard Nimoy (age 82 in 2014; "Mr. Spock" on 'Star Trek') has lung disease (chronic obstructive), he informed Pers Morgan on CNN on Feb.10, 2014. He described himself as "a champion smoker." He died in March, 2015. His death will be searched for in Torah Code for a later book.

David Brenner, American comedian, age 78, died on about March 15, 2014, of cancer. The radio and television reports did not specify what kind of terminal cancer caused his death, but might be reported later. When more on his cause of death is released, a Bible Code Matrix could be generated, and included in a future, expanded edition of this Volume.

Francis Crick, co-discoverer of the DNA molecule, died at age 88 in 2004, of colon cancer. In an expanded edition of this Volume a Bible Code Matrix could be included showing such a search result.

Also, 'swine flu,' as the virus H1N1 made a comeback in the 2013-14 season, killing several people in the U.S.. Later, a search for this disease and its victims in the Bible Code could be done, along with the Key word as 'malignancy' (as used in this volume), along with terms like 'swine, flu, virus, death,' and even the names of the victims who died, and maybe even the location (state and/or city) and date (at least the year of their death; with the proviso explained in Appendix 1 explaining how and why our calendar is so inaccurate).

"Life grows out of death, and death from life." (Eric Wilson, *Against Happiness*, p.44)

Part 1: Accidents – Celebrities:

'Ranker.com' is used here as a source for biographical information on prominent people.

Car Crash (Princess Diana, Isadora Duncan), **Fire** (astronaut Virgil 'Gus' Grissom), **Plane Crash** (John Denver, Robert F. Kennedy, Jr.), **Skiing** (Sonny Bono).

Princess Diana: see Fig.1, in which '-cess' of 'Pr(i)ncess' is phonetic as '-ses.' Her first name is phonetically clear when pronounced without the 'i.' Paris, the city in which the horrific tunnel crash occurred was not found encoded, as with four letters, but is found broken into two phonetic parts. While 'Pr(i)–' was not found encoded close to the Key or the '-cess' [-ses], it _was_ found encoded three times, as shown in the one long Matrix cut up to fit onto a page, as shown below. The Hebrew dictionary spelling of 'tunnel' has 3 different spellings, all 5 letters long; only one is found encoded, in Matrix #1 of the 5 found of the Key (phonetic of 'car crash', using Hebrew letters). Since only Matrix 3 is shown here, we don't see the word 'tunnel' encoded; see Fig.1.

Isadora Duncan: choreographer and trail-blazing dancer, 1877 - 1927; 'car crash' as the Key is transliterated (Hebrew letters for English letter sound equivalents). Year of crash, 1927, was searched for but not found encoded. Later perhaps the location of the deadly car crash will be researched and found, wherever it occurred. Fig.2, Matrix 1 of the 5 found of the Key is used below showing the most found results in the most compact array within the Matrices found. There was a 28% increase in traffic accidents in the U.S., from drug-use over decade of about 2002 to 2012.

Virgil 'Gus' Grissom: NASA astronaut, born in 1926, died on Jan. 27, 1967 in a fire that engulfed the Apollo spacecraft on the launch pad. He died along with two other astronauts, Ed White, and Roger Chaffee. 'ApoloShip' as the Key is transliterated. See Fig.3. On left of upper part of the Matrix note the neat trick of crossing the two parts of his encoded last name (phonetically with only one 's'). Is this a possible semiotic symbol signifier – wiping out a life by 'crossing out' a name? The depths of encoded meanings buried in what is being uncovered here cannot be pre-judged, because the intellect and technological abilities of the Torah encoders are far beyond human comprehension. Satinover points out the NSA has concluded that humans are not at this time capable of encoding such a large text as the Torah to the vast extent as has been found by Bible Code researchers. More 'fire' and more 'Vir-' could be labeled here. The Hebrew calendar year HC5730 found encoded goes from mid-September 1969, 2.75 years later than the date of the accident in our Gregorian calendar (which is too low in its count; see Appendix 1).

John Denver: singer, song-writer, in 1997 died in the crash of his experimental airplane. Where this occurred and the type of aircraft needs to be found out and searched for to see if they're also Torah-encoded along with what is found in Matrix 1 of 1 found of the phonetic Key; see Fig.4.

John F. Kennedy, Jr.: son of JFK and publishing executive. Date, and place (other than just off the New England coast; could GPS coordinates be found Torah-encoded?) Need to be researched and searched for in Bible Code. To left of part of Matrix 1 of 1 shown below ('PlaneCrash' as phonetic Key) are encoded 2 'death' and 1 'John.' Apparently there was fog along the northeast coastline he was flying without instruments, and darkness descended as he searched for the airport. He apparently became disoriented, and the plane ran out of fuel. No spelling of 'fog' is found encoded with this Key, but the relevance of that might be totally immaterial, since the encoded Torah seems to reveal what occurred throughout all of human history, not necessarily including any contributing causes as to why. See Fig.5.

Sonny Bono: singer and entertainer, partner of the singer 'Cher'. He died in a skiing accident near Lake Tahoe, California on Jan. 4, 1998; crashed into a tree and died from the head injury of severe concussion. The odds of finding the Key, 'SonyBono,' encoded at the found skip of only 383 letters is *less than 1 in a million*, according to the program's automatic calculation.

Fatalities at U.S. ski resorts have remained at about 40 per year for some time now. The greater popularity of wearing helmets does not seem to have made a difference in attempts to reduce the number of such deadly accidents. See Fig.6.

Part 1: Accidents – Stars

Car Crash (James Dean, Ryan Dunn, Paul Walker, Grace Kelly), **Drowning** (Natalie Wood), **Fire** (Linda Darnell), **Plane Crash** (Ricky Nelson).

James Dean: he died in a car crash on September 30, 1955, near Shandon, California, in his Porsche Spyder, ran head-on at 85 miles per hour into Donald Turnupseed's (a Cal Poly student in San Luis Obispo) 1950 Ford Tudor coupe. Hebrew calendar year 5710 goes from about mid-September 1949 to mid-September 1950, which is about 60 months earlier than the deadly crash itself. The year of the crash HC 5716 wasn't found encoded here. His first name is found only as 'Jim,' not in any version of 'James,' phonetic or otherwise. The full spelling of 'California' (in 3 parts) is found encoded here but only 'Cali-' is shown; 19 '-for-' and 14 '-nia' are found encoded. See Figs.7, 8 and 9.

Ryan Dunn: age 34, driving his Porsche 911 GT3, crashed and burned on June 20, 2011, on Route 322 in Penn. He was a star on the tv hit show 'Jackass.' See Figs. 10 and 11.

Paul Walker: movie star actor, born in 1973, died in a car crash (type of car?) on November 30, 2013, in Santa Clara, California. Date or year not found encoded here at the short skip to find the Key. More '-ker' could be labeled in the Matrix. To left of Key note 3-way use of encoded -P- in 3 'Paul' found encoded. Don't try such encoding at home, you'll hurt yourself. See Fig.12.

Grace Kelly: car crash in Monaco on September 13, 1982. She might have strangled from a long scarf she was wearing that got caught in a spinning hub-cap protrusion. The year found encoded, HC 5740 (1979-80), is about 24 months 'off.' While 'Grs' (only phonetic of 'Grace' found encoded here)) means 'expelled' in Hebrew, we take the best phonetic version. And the -ce- of her first name as the 's' sound is here found as the Hebrew letter *Shin*. See Fig.13.

Natalie Wood: In 1981 she drowned at night after slipping off the yacht moored in Catalina she shared with her husband Robert Wagner and a friend, Christopher Walken. The two men were in the main cabin and didn't notice her absence until it was far too late. She had <u>fallen</u> to her <u>death</u> and <u>drown</u>(ed) – specific words in Hebrew found in the Matrix shown below. In Matrix 1 of 2 of 'Drown' as the Key we see encoded: 'Natalie, Wood, drown, fallen, death, death.' In upper right the fact that 'death' and 'Wood' (diagonal) share an encoded letter should give us pause to ponder the truth of such insistent facts out of the mysterious mouth of Yahweh. In this Matrix, more could be labeled to right of the screen print, with 'death' and 'Wood.' See Fig.14.

In Matrix 2 of 2 (Fig.15) we see encoded: 'Nat-alie, Wood, drown, Cata-lina.' Here we see a Torah-code Matrix revealing <u>where</u> she died, and very close to <u>when</u> she died. '-alie' wraps around from column 11 to column 1, to column 96 to column 86, with a skip of 9 letters. Look at a Matrix like a scroll wrapped around a tube. I cut the Matrix print and moved that right-side section to the left, so it fits on a page. Five of year 1979-80 (HC 5740) are found encoded in Matrix 2. One is not shown but starts 3 columns to right of the Key and 2 rows below it, with a skip of 6 letters between highlighted letters that spell out the year. Hebrew is the only language that uses letters for numbers. The year found here ends in mid-Sept 1980, so is as little as 4 months 'off' of her death date, the specific date of the accident (not found in my research). The Hebrew Calendar is a lunar calendar, as is the Muslim calendar. See Fig.15.

Linda Darnell: film actress (her line in 1949 movie 'Fallen Angel' was beyond memorable – 'Why don't you leave me alone, you make sick'), died from burns sustained in house fire April 10, 1965 (age 41.5), Glenview, Illinois. Born October 16, 1923, Dallas, Texas. Note in Matrix, top left center, 'fire,' 'house' and 'death' <u>touch each other</u>, the vertical 'house' <u>sharing a letter</u> with 'death.' Even her name (as the vertical Key) <u>shares a letter</u> with 'fire.' The Torah encoders are beyond serious in what they have secretly buried in the Torah's text. See Fig.16.

Ricky Nelson: age 45, actor and singer, died in a plane crash of his DC-3, near DeKalb, Texas, on December 3, 1985. Also killed were his fiancee and four others/ members of his band, and his sound man. The plane was over 40 years old and beset with engine trouble. In news reports he is called 'Rick,' not 'Ricky' (which might have been reserved only for his tv show). Note to right of the Key in the Matrix below the 'r' in diagonal Hebrew word for 'sing' <u>shares</u> that 'r' as first letter of his first name. The 'y' with that name wasn't found encoded, consistent with what he was actually called. More could be labeled here but then it would be too crowded to read clearly. See Fig.17.

Part 2: Murders – Jodi Arias stabbed Travis Alexander; O.J. Simpson stabbed Nicole Brown Simpson and Ronald Goldman; John Lennon was shot in New York City (text only, no Matrix or Figure).

'Stabbing,' kill, blade, death, murder. The Key's spelling is transliterated phonetically from English letter sounds into Hebrew letter sounds. As many or more of these elements are also found encoded in Matrix 2 of 2 (not shown). See Fig.18 for Matrix 1 of 2.

'Stabbing,' cut, throat, blade, kill, massacre, carnage, decapitation, homicide. See Fig.19.

Jodi Arias murdered Travis Alexander on June 4, 2008, at his home in Mesa, Arizona. She stabbed him almost 70 times and then shot him in the face. In Phoenix, Arizona Jodi was convicted of first degree murder on May 8, 2013, after weeks of televised trial. She testified on the witness stand that she killed Travis in self-defense. Found in Matrix 1 of 2 are: 'Stab(b)ing, Jodi, Ari-ias, murderer, kill, murder, June (Hebrew month of *Sivan*). See Fig.20

Jodi Arias as accidental mythic figure – In the trial of Jodi Arias' murder of Travis Alexander we confront our society's obsession with sexual violence. If her baser motive was revenge for her perceived anal rape while still in sacramental, ritual clothing just after her initiation into the Mormon faith, then her choice of stabbing him to death while he was showering (purifying his body of the violation he had committed, washing off the sin of sodomy) was symbolically reflected in her drenching-bathing him in his own blood, using the knife to penetrate his body as he had used his erect penis as a weapon to penetrate her body, to violate her trust, and spoil the sanctity of her religious conversion.

In the sacrificial sanctity of blood she bathed him in the ritual of defilement and humiliation proportional to her own sense of violation and depraved servitude. A blood bath commensurate with the bath she needed to feel sufficient retribution. Did the 29 knife wounds she inflicted on him nearly match the 29 penile strokes it took him to ejaculate in her anus? Was she counting, even subconsciously? Probably no jury member will think to ask such a question.

The wall-to-wall media coverage of the trial illustrates how media and "murder have intersected in the sexual politics of culture." (Phrase from *Labyrinth Books* catalog description, March 2013, p.31, of *Lustmord: Sexual Murder in Weimar Germany*, by Maria Tatar, 1997, Princeton Univ. Press).

Jodi Arias as an Angel of Death – "... stabbed him 30 times, and then shot him to death. The stabbings were to inflict as much pain as possible before he died." (Witness in *Law and Order* tv series, episode 'Castoff,' 1998).

As an Angel of Death, Jodi was only continuing the ritual of religious initiation that Travis had culminated in his own way with forced (or at least involuntary) anal intercourse as his view of her conversion to his religion, giving her a clear idea what she was in for if she stayed with him. Jodi's transformation from subservient girlfriend to Angel of Death came when she decided to exact retributive revenge for his degradation of her. She reversed the power of ritual back on him with a finality reflecting the *petit mort* he experienced as he ejaculated in her lower colon.

She decided not to marry him because he had violated the celestial contract that would have allowed such a sacred commitment. She wrote in her journal: "There's something not right with that boy."

Travis Alexander: "Stab(b)ing, Mesa, Ariz-ona, *Sivan* (June)." In Matrix 1 of 2 found of the Key. 'X' sound in Hebrew is made of 'k' and then 's' letters. More parts except 'Mesa' and 'Alek-' are to left and right of the screen print. More could be labeled here. This is the same Matrix (#1 of 2) in which Jodi's name is found encoded, with "murderer, kill, murder." *Sivan* (June) is to the left, off this screen print; the month in which he was killed. The year was not found encoded; also, a search for the year taking into consideration the calendar adjustment explained in Appendix 1 was not done. See Fig.21.

O.J. Simpson: ex-football player, murdered his ex-or-estranged wife Nicole Brown Simpson, mother of their two mixed-race children, and her friend Ron Goldman, in Brentwood, Calif., in 1994. 'Brown' is from program's Hebrew dictionary, spelling 3 of 3. 'Nicol(e)' is found encoded only in Matrix #2 of the two found of the Key, 'Stab(b)ing.' See Fig.22.

A jury famously found him 'not guilty' of murder and he walked free. Whites across the country were astonished, given the overwhelming evidence and apparently insurmountable case the DA had methodically and competently presented, and blacks rejoiced from coast to coast, cheering the verdict, accentuating the racial divide in America, and exposing in this most famous case to date the hidden race war going on in the U.S. – FBI statistics (presented by Mr. Buchanan in a tv interview) show that blacks commit crimes against whites out of proportion to their population by a factor of 14, compared to the crimes whites commit against blacks.

'Gold' transliterated was not found encoded, but spelling 2 of 2 in the program's Hebrew dictionary was found and is shown in Matrix #2, as <u>Fig.23</u>.

Matrix #1 also has all these parts encoded, but in different and denser array, and also shows 'Br(e) nt-wood' encoded; -'wood' is from program's dictionary, spelling 4 of 5; <u>see Fig.24.</u>

See print of Matrix #2 for other 'OJSi–mps-son encoded with the Key.

John Lennon: shot to death on December 8, 1980 in New York City (NYC) by Mark David Chapman (MDC). Essential facts of this murder are found encoded in Matrix 2 of 7 found of the Key ("Jo(h)nLen(n)on"), from Gen.1:1 to Numbers 4:29; skip 11,455 letters to find the Key encoded. Matrix shows: **Jo(h)nLen(n)on, USA, assassination, NYC, HC5741** (1980), [by] **MDC."** The date of Dec. 8 wasn't searched for. How did the Torah encoders know of this murder and the *three initials* of <u>where</u> it would take place, and <u>who</u> would commit the act, much less in what year it would occur so many millennia in the future? Is it a matter of us dealing with an anti-entropic oracle text able somehow to defy the one-way arrow of time and the basic laws of thermodynamics, or did they write the 'script' and are in control?

Benito Mussolini: ministerial president of Italy, was killed by a mob at the end of WWII. Matrix 8 of 34 found of the Key ('Muslini'), from Gen.11:11 to Numbers 9:18; skip 9745 letters to find the Key encoded, show: **Muslini, ministerial, president, murdered, HC5705** (1945). <u>See Fig.25.</u> Same results found in Matrix 17, from Leviticus 26:44 to Joshua 4:16, skip 6362 letters.

Part 3: Overdoses – Philip Seymour Hoffman, Marilyn Monroe, others, Michael Jackson.

There are about 38,000 overdose deaths in the U.S. every 365 days. Individuals' notoriety on the basis of stardom or celebrity are covered extensively by the commercial news media. Most ODs of course go unreported, mostly because of apathy and the anonymity of the victim.

Felony drug arrests were down 32% in New York City from 2008 to 2012, so the police arresting 3 or 4 street-level drug dealers in the Hoffman case was a news-worthy exception. Of course, when there's an Oscar award-winning Hollywood actor involved, the political pressure to make an arrest and charge a dealer with contributing to the death becomes a priority above and beyond the usual scandal.

The White House and the U.S. Attorney General Eric Holder advocating early release of tens of thousands of federal drug-offense-charged criminals from prison doesn't necessarily help the safety of America's neighborhoods and young people. That policy sounds like part of President Obama's announced and clear goal and intent to "fundamentally transform the United States of America." The rule of law is fundamental to the Constitutional democracy, so undermining the rule of law, changing prison sentences on an ad-hoc and ex-post facto basis, and circumventing Congress and the courts does help to weaken America from the inside.

About 3000 people OD on heroin every year in the U.S.. Since I could find all their names encoded in the sacred text of the Torah, each year I'd have a 3000-page long book, at one name per page found in the Key Death Matrix. If a book publisher wants to fund such a an annual compilation, I could hire and train a staff to produce the documents.

Other opiates (poppy flower derived; the flowers mostly from Afghanistan), including prescription drugs (like 'oxycotin'), account for the balance of the yearly 38,000 total killed in America by accidental overdosing. I could also produce a complete research report of all those names found Torah-encoded, along with what they OD'd on, where they did it, and perhaps even the date. That report would be about 38,000 pages long each year.

The heroin epidemic in America has arisen partly because of the tighter restrictions on doctors prescribing pain medications in new pain management regimes, making such meds more expensive and harder to come by. Filling the demand gap is cheaper heroin. The prior heroin epidemic was in the 1970s and 1980s.

The total dead currently in Ods is greater than from auto accidents (about 38,000 a year, down from near 50,000 decades ago) and suicides. Mixing drugs has increased the OD death rate. Drinking alcohol with opiates increases the risk of overdosing.

Heroin now is a global epidemic. 80% can be sourced to Afghanistan, where 5% of the population is addicted. Peak levels of poppy production occurred in 2014 in Afghanistan. The Taliban is funding its insurgency through poppy growth, trade and sale.

Confiscation of heroin on the Mexican border has recently greatly increased. Labs have grown in recent years and while the quality is below par, production is way up and prices on the west coast are very low.

Philip Seymour Hoffman: actor, movie star, born 1947, died Feb. 2, 2014, age 47, in his New York City apartment, of a heroin drug overdose. He was found in the bathroom with a needle in his arm. 50 bags of heroin were found in the apartment, and 20 used syringes. The prescription drug "Vivance" was also found, a psychological stimulant drug used for withdrawal. The heroin he used might have been combined with a cancer pain-reducing drug, which makes the heroin 100 times more powerful. Hundreds of people in the U.S. have died from this in recent years.

He was in 15 movies, and was playing the lead in a stage production of Arthur Miller's "Death of a Salesman." His films included "Mission Impossible 3," and in 2005 was the lead in "Capote," for which he won Academy Award for Best Actor. He was in rehab in 2013 after relapsing in 2012. He was also in "Red Dragon" (2002), with Anthony Hopkins and Edward Norton (as Hannibal).

A later edition of this book might include a Bible Code Matrix of search results for him.

Marilyn Monroe: actress, movie star. Her death in August 1962, thought to be a suicide at that time, shocked the world. The coroner's report stated that her death was due to a massive overdose of Nambutal capsules. But what about the discrepancies between the official report and the eyewitness accounts of the people who were there at the scene of her death – friends, her housekeeping staff, police officers, and doctors? And what about the forensic evidence that disappeared between the time of her death and the coroner's report being issued? (See book jacket of Matthew Smith's 2004 book *Marilyn's Last Words*).

"Answers come in all shapes and sizes, however, and one man's answer sometimes presents itself as another man's question." (Matthew Smith, 2004, p.156). Also see his other book, *The Men Who Murdered Marilyn*; also see R.F. Slatzer's 1975 *The Life and Curious Death of Marilyn Monroe*; also see Milo Speriglo's 1982 *Marilyn Monroe: Murder Cover-Up*, and his 1986 *The Marilyn Conspiracy*.

Marilyn Monroe's internal organs were not only examined at the autopsy, but removed and not found later. What happened to them and why? Wouldn't they have retained some of the barbiturates that didn't go through the digestive system? She died of a drug overdose on August 4, 1962, slipped into a coma and wasn't able to wake up. Her diary and a note were stolen from her house to stop a scandal about her connection to RFK and JFK from getting into the public arena and the media.

According to researcher and author Matthew Smith, in his 2004 book, *Marilyn's Last Words – Her Secret Tapes and Mysterious Death*, she was murdered, administered lethal drugs in an undetectable way (read book to find out how; the method was too vile, venal and revolting to describe here).

A later edition of this Volume would include a Bible Code search Matrix about her death.

Other names that would be included in that expanded Volume would be famous people who also died of drug overdoses, such as: Anna Nicole Smith, Brian Adams, John Belushi, Elvis Presley, Cory Monteith, Chris Farley, Judy Garland, Jimi Hendrix, Janis Joplin, Whitney Houston, and Amy Winehouse.

Michael Jackson: a singer and dancer in pop music, died on June 25, 2009 of an overdose of 'propofal,' an anaesthetic provided by his doctor (who was later convicted and imprisoned for a time). In the Matrix 1 of 1 presented here twice, the Key, 'overdose,' is transliterated. 'Michael' is phonetic as 'M(i)kel.'

There are 5 other Matrices that could be examined, all with shorter skips to find the Key encoded, other than the one presented her. Those smaller Matrices hold less information about his death than does the one shown below as <u>Fig.26 and Fig.27</u>.

Note below in left center of Fig.26, his last name touches the '-fol' of the drug that killed him. Three more 'Jack-' could be labeled here. <u>See Fig.26.</u>

Found encoded in Fig.27 are 'sing,' 'dance,' the year of his death (2009; Hebrew Calendar year 5770), 'death,' and another spelling of 'death.' These two encoded Hebrew spellings of 'death' almost touch the prophetic Key, 'Overdose,' the cause of his death.

The 4 elegantly intertwined 'death' in the top part of the Matrix (2 on the left, diagonal, sharing letters, and 2 crossing the top part of the Key, also sharing letters) are testament to the amazing encoding abilities of the Torah encrypters so many thousands of years ago. <u>See Fig.27.</u>

Part 4: Suicides – Ava Braun, Adolf Hitler, Ernest Hemingway, Queen Cleopatra, Brynn Hartman, Ryan Jenkins, Ruslana Korshunova.

Ava Braun: She killed herself with poison, along with her lover Adolf Hitler, in their Berlin bunker in 1945, as Russian troops were advancing in the city near the end of the WWII. On the right side of the Matrix below, between columns 1 and 43 (off screen) are found 'Ava, Bra-aun, death.' <u>See Fig.28.</u>

Adolf Hitler: He committed suicide in his Berlin bunker in 1945 by poisoning himself. In the Matrix 1 of 1 found of the Key, 'suicide,' to avoid searching for only 2 letters, and 'o' is added to the 2nd half of his first name. 'Suicide' is from program's Hebrew dictionary, spelling 1 of 2. There are

62 of matrices with this Key but all have larger skipping to find the Key encoded. At the skip of the Matrix shown here, only 149 letters, only one Matrix if found. To the right, between columns 3 and 38 (off screen), all tightly clustered (note they would be very close to the vertical Key when the Matrix is wrapped around a cylinder, just left of the Key) are 'Ado-olf' and 'Hit-ler.' See Fig.29.

Queen Cleopatra: ... of Alexandria, Egypt, committed suicide in 30 B.C. by being bitten by an asp, a small, venomous snake. 'Asp' is transliterated. 'Venom' is program's Hebrew dictionary spelling 2 of 3. 'Egyptian' (program's Hebrew dictionary spelling 1 of 1) is found 6 times in Matrix #2, but none in Matrix #1, shown below. Note in upper right center, diagonal 'asp' and vertical 'venom' share an encoded letter. Put nothing of such profound simplicity and elegance beyond the Torah encoders. Several more 'venom' and 'snake' could be labeled. See Fig.30.

Brynn Hartman: she shot her husband, the comedian Phil Hartman, as he slept, then she shot herself, in May 1998. The month and day of her suicide weren't searched for, and the two Hebrew Calendar (HC) years that contain 1998 weren't found encoded, but the HC year starting only 16 months later *was* found encoded, HC5760 (goes from mid-September 1999 to mid-Sept 2000). Some more 'shooting' could be labeled in the Matrix below. See Fig.31.

Ernest Hemingway: American, Nobel-Prize-winning novelist, born in 1899, shot himself in 1961. The year was not found encoded in Matrix 1 of 1 found of the Key, 'suicide,' shown below as Fig.32.

25 more 'Ern-' could be labeled here, and 62 more 'Hem-.' 50 more 'shooting' (program's dictionary spelling 2 of 3) could be labeled here -- the dramatic point is made by the Torah encoders by putting 2 with letters *touching*, one so close to the vertical Key 'suicide' you can almost smell the gun powder.

When 1961 in Hebrew Calendar years 5721 (1960-1) and 5722 (1961-2) are searched for at the maximum skip allowed looking for the Key, 2 are found of each. The maximum search skip allowed (determined by the spelling length of the Key, in this case 7 letters, program's dictionary Hebrew spelling 1 of 2, and the range of the biblical text chosen to search, in this case the *whole* Torah, from Gen.1:1 to Deuteronomy 34:12). At this maximum skip search of 50,800 letters, 63 Keys are found encoded. In Matrix #14 (with its skip of10,059 letters to find the Key encoded), HC5721 (1960-1) is found encoded, along with all the other factors shown in Matrix #43 (with its smallest skip of the 63 Matrices found, shown below as Matrix 1 of 1, with its skip of 149 letters to find the Key encoded. See Fig.32.

'HC5721' is also found in Matrix #25, with its skip of 18,883 letters to find the Key encoded. Matrix #34 has 'HC5722' encoded; skipping 23,010 letters to find the Key encoded.

Ryan Jenkins: born Feb 8, 1977, died August 23, 2009, age 32; reality tv star, hanged himself with a belt in his motel in Canada, 5 days after the body of his fiance/girlfriend was discovered (she'd been murdered).

The death year was found encoded, as HC5770 (2009-10) but only in Matrix #1 of 2 found of the Key, 'suicide.' Only Matrix #2 was printed here, as Fig.33.

'Belt' (transliterated) is found just above the Key, on row #1, with a skip of 8 letters. Some would say it's meaningless that in the lower part of the Matrix on row 11 his last name and 'hanged' are found encoded *touching* each other, and even *share* a letter. And his first name is only 4 letters away. Perhaps fate comes in many configurations, and this is one of them, at least as found in the encoded original word of Yahweh several thousand years ago.

No doubt 'motel' and maybe even its name and town, and 'Can-ada' could be found here.

Ruslana Korshunova: born July 2, 1987, died June 28, 2008, age 20 (only 4 days from her 21st birthday). Kazakh supermodel of Russian heritage, fell from 9th floor apartment balcony in New York City (NYC).

More 'NYC' could be labeled in the Matrix shown below (2 of 2 found of Key), but note in lower part on column 1 the *shared* 'N' of vertical 'NYC' (6-skip) and 'n' of her last name (horizontal, 2-skip, on row 15). See Fig.34.

Afterword

"If our questions of [life and death] are to hold out the promise of self-knowledge that [birth itself has allowed for], we can't ask them outside of history." (See Gopnick, p.8).

Apparently the future has already been recorded, in a sacred text of 304,805 Hebrew letters, in the Torah. All of human history and events on the Earth are found encoded in the Books and verses from Genesis to Deuteronomy, or in the larger Torah, the whole Hebrew Bible. Samples have been included in this volume and are described in the Book List titles offered.

This process presents us with an ethical conundrum of framing a relevant perspective that reveals a truth not immediately ready to disclose itself ... illuminating the possibility of complex knowledge hidden in the mind of God that we can safely reveal in a format like this book – an exfoliation of evidence, perception and intuition ... leading to a vibrant document, interpreting the evidence gleaned from the broken tongue of Yahweh.

Silent, we stand in awe, waiting for the next sky to fall, the next world to dissolve in an instant as we are transported to the eternal presence of the source of all Being, and again walk in a state of Grace. This strange occurrence was experienced by the author in Milwaukee in about 1985, when he lived there for a year.

This is God's Secret Code of Death embedded in the encrypted text of the sacred Torah, making the detective work itself a kind of sacred quest, a blessed calling, or at least a determined dedication of a sort of lone monk in the desert battling every day for a morsel of truth.

We the living bear witness to the vengeance, vengeance under the guise of blood cult sacrifice orchestrated by an agency beyond human comprehension, orchestrated by an intelligence beyond the strictures of time, and with the technical ability to encrypt a large text, the Torah made of 304,805 Hebrew letters, that apparently predicted the future as of about 3500 years ago. J. Satinover (see References) cites conclusions by computer experts and the NSA that humans do not have at this time the ability to encrypt such a text to the deep extent as found in Bible Code research. He tells of NSA personnel, after delving into Bible Codes, taking early retirement and moving themselves and their families to Israel for further, deeper study.

We are witness to a secret on the tongue of God, a secret called Death. The celestial reckonings of the God of Death, meting out the mysterious justice of mortality in ways we never would in our blind ethics rendering the helpless and defenseless mere pawns in a king's whimsy of crass politics and the glory and survival of his people.

All human wars in recorded history – the dead named by Yahweh at least 3500 years ago. Later volumes in the war series will search for those names in all the major wars and battles throughout human history, their full names to be found encoded in the Five Books of Moses. A few volumes now available in the Book List go some distance in fulfilling that goal.

How can we escape the naming, and thus perhaps escape death itself? In what sacred text prior to the Torah might be encoded the names of the dead in earlier wars, or are they also encoded in the Torah, and all we need to know are the names of those wars and battles? For example, in my book on **Assassinations,** ancient Egyptian names of those assassinated 4000 years ago were found encoded in the Torah (names known even before it was presented to the Hebrew people), as 'assassinated.'

Misplaced assumptions and unknown unknowns get in the way of creating clarity in our understanding of the necessary parameters for establishing knowledge in this enterprise. The causality issue is enlightening of what we don't know. Dissecting the matrix of space and time in order to tell the future exposes a utilitarian algorithm not used for centuries in the seance parlors of the spiritualist underworld.

Regarding terror attacks -- among the top 31 terrorists in the world today, only one is a non-Muslim. An infidel is defined in Islam as any non-Muslim. A verse in the Koran says: "Kill the infidels wherever you find them." Muslims believe there are no innocent infidels, partly because if they were not anti-Muslim they would not be infidels, and since they have had opportunities to convert (three warnings are required in the Koran), their rejection is a constant reminder of their hostility to Islam and to the teachings of the Prophet (praise be upon him and his 9-year old, favorite wife, Aisha).

Moral equivalency of victims such as children, women and old men ignores intention – jihad terrorists aim for such civilians and hide among Muslim women and children, while the U.S. military aims at war targets and tries to avoid collateral civilian damage. Moral equivalency of "freedom fighter" and terrorist ignores the fact that terrorists don't believe in freedom as we understand it in Western civilization, and don't fight as such – setting IEDs and hiding among civilians to avoid battle engagement is not fighting in any traditional military sense.

"If your life is not on the line, it's not real." Factory Five spokesman; kit cars, 'Megakits,' 2011, on The Speed Channel.

The reality is that our lives are on the line every moment of every day, we just don't know what Key to look for in the Book of Death in order to tell when and where and how our number will be up. There may be a work-around that could potentially avoid that problem. The author is exploring various approaches to this problem.

The Torah is a text of coded secrets resulting in multi-dimensional Matrices when searched for connections and explanations of how to read reality. Although cracking open Joseph Chilton Pierce's "cosmic egg" might reveal a hidden reality of immeasurable scale, we are still left with our inescapable limitations restricting our assumptions about what is possible. Are we permitted to peer across the divide between living and dead?

Who will object to these findings and on what will those objections be based? The reaction of some is that these names of events, places and the dead, especially *all* these names, *should* not be found in small sections of the Torah, and *could* not reasonably be found encoded, much less found encoded closely bunched together around the 'Key' word, because such findings would be *far* beyond any reasonable expectation of chance, and thus would not be possible, based on a rational analysis of how language works.

Thus preconceived notions can create a blind spot of denial in which what is seen in black and white is not believed as true or as a legitimate outcome of a standard procedure in a research discipline that is about 900 years old. Objections within that field of investigation will come partly from rejecting the application of phonetic deconstruction of names into their syllables, as if the rule of meaningfulness from the phenomenon of observed *proximity* doesn't apply to those constituent parts of words uttered as whole sounds.

The dead are in the Word, their names broken within the encoded text, exactly as spoken on the broken tongue of Yahweh. Have the ancient encoders of that Sacred Word been able to break down the barrier not only of space and time but of consciousness and quantum being, focusing on an essence of humanity yet unidentified by us so far (leaving the question of 'soul' aside for now in our current effort to more clearly appraise our situation)?

The alphabet accommodates the tongue, so we see what is encoded in Holy Word when the tripping of the Sacred Tongue is phonetically and faithfully de-constructed to fit the ear of YHWH and the mouth of Moses.

Conclusion

Notes on Meaning

"Sometimes in order to see the light you have to risk the darkness."
(the inventor of Pre-Crime, in the movie "Minority Report," 2002)

As to the question, 'What does it mean?' I can only suggest we examine some of the preconceptions imbedded in such a question and look carefully and thoroughly at what would it mean for these discoveries to mean anything at all, taking into consideration an examination of *meaning* itself, beyond the epistemological implications. Assuming that they do, we can explore the repercussions of the implications of what we might see implied here.

Confining our concerns to the meaning of these findings *qua* 'meaning' would be merely melodramatic. Through the Bible-Torah Code search process, applied to significant, historical events, we can curate them, synthesize the encoded data, and analyze the composite results, and finally put their implications in the context of the greater journey of humankind upon the Earth.

As Ogdon and Richards state in their 1923 Preface to their book *The Meaning of Meaning – A Study of the Influence of Language Upon Thought and of the Science of Symbolism*, "language is the most important of all the instruments of civilization." And thus we look through the lens of language in this Torah Code mystery to try and understand what it means to be human.

Bertrand Russell, on page 47 of his *Principles of Mathematics*, says: "Words all have meaning, in the simple sense that they are symbols which stand for something other than themselves. ... Thus meaning, in the sense in which words have meaning, is irrelevant to logic." (See p.273 of Ogdon and Richards).

In an attempt at meta-understanding of the meaning of what is found encoded in the Torah, we can begin to appreciate the layers of language embedded within language that hold long-standing truths bursting at the proverbial seams to break free and announce themselves in a song of deeper understanding of what drips from the broken tongue of Yahweh. Gathered here we have presented some samples of that potential in hopes of them shedding light on what is possible to understand of what is secretly buried inside this sacred text.

"The odds against chance are dropping fast."
Jack (Harrison Ford) in movie, *Patriot Games* (1992)

Calculating the probability of finding all these encoded terms close to each other and in *one* Matrix, and all close to the Key (multiply each successive probability with each other to find out what the odds are against pure chance; will be exceedingly small), shows an exponential decrease against chance each time we find such Torah search results. Coincidence plays an increasingly smaller role as we continue to explore this phenomenon of encoded historical secrets. Satinover points out that Torah Code researchers have concluded that the encoding of the text was not only far beyond chance but was done *intentionally.*

"The connection between the calligraphy and the sword is a mystery. The mystery can be explained only by those who can perceive the connection between them." (Martial arts master Jet Li, Master Lin the assassin, in Chinese movie *Hero*, 2002, directed by Zhang Yimou, who also directed "Raise the Red Lantern").

Not only has the connection been explained by the author, but the demonstrably valid conclusion can be drawn based on the explained connection (between Hebrew in the Torah [the calligraphy] and murder [the sword]) that God is not squeamish.

"The gods are worthless as protectors." ('Snow' to the assassin, Jet Li). 'The brush and the sword share the same principles." (Brother Sword to Snow). So the Word and Death share the same principles, are intuitively connected through tongue, breath and mortality.

"Men and sword become interchangeable." (The King to Master Lin, Jet Li). "A warrior's ultimate act is to lay down his sword." (Master Lin to the King after he stabs him from behind with the king's sword).

The Glory of the Word becomes a Death Nell for those enshrined in the Death Matrix of the Holy text. Only non-identity could save any of us from that fate, but since even DNA is the essence of individual identity that can be delineated and transliterated into corresponding Hebrew letters in proper sequence (A-T, G-C) in full expression for individual identification, there is no escape along that front. We realize there is no escape from Yahweh already having called us to oblivion. The only differentiating factor is timing, the when of the end, and that is unknown and cannot be predicted with much degree of certainty. Even suicides are not always successful. Yahweh's prohibition against people trying to see into the future is spelled out in Deuteronomy 18: 10-14. Given the modern superstitious mind-set, it is worth reading.

How do we explain this Bible Code phenomenon? Edward O. Wilson has argued that "there is intrinsically only one class of explanation. It traverses the scales of space, time, and complexity to unite the disparate facts of the disciplines of consilience, the perception of a seamless web of cause and effect." (on p.266 of his 1998 book *Consilience: the Unity of Knowledge*).

If I could repeal the encoded Word of God, I would, but His will cannot be avoided, negated, countered or neutralized, so the carnage among humans will continue. YHWH long ago tried to wipe all humans off the surface of the Earth through the flooding power of the Deluge, the Great Flood. After this attempt failed, Yahweh promised not to use water again to try and kill all humans. What purpose, in YHWH's mind, does a "flood of blood" serve? Is it a substitute for a "flood of water" but still vengeance upon humanity for continuing to offend YHWH in some way, perhaps just by existing?

Genesis 6-9 tells the Deluge story of the Great Flood, a devastating worldwide catastrophe that occurred in about 2348 BC, according to one calculation (see Wikipedia). While apparently intended by YHWH as a prelude to a new beginning for mankind, according to one interpretation explaining why Noah and his family were saved, in order to re-populate the Earth. But Noah was not warned by Yahweh of the coming Deluge, nor did Yahweh instruct him how to build the Ark – a voice behind a wall did that (see Sitchin for the identity of who that was). And repopulating the Earth would not be possible from such a small genetic base as only one family, even if incest were sanctioned and encouraged.

"Logic in its final perfection is insane." (Andrea Nye, 1990, in the closing sentence of her essay, "A Thought Like a Hammer: the Logic of Totalitarianism," the penultimate chapter of a work devoted to just that arresting proposition; see Norris, 2006, p.23).

What C. Paglia says of Lewis Carroll's view of manners and social laws being disconnected from values could apply to how we need to evaluate the import of these mysterious Torah Matrices – "They have a mathematical beauty but no moral meaning: they are *absurd*. But this absurdity is predicated not on a democratic notion of their relativism but on their arbitrary, divine incomprehensibility." (Paglia, 1991, p.553)

Indeed, how can we possibly penetrate the sacred word in any way that is truly, inherently, objectively meaningful? Having broken the Hebrew text's code, we still lack the probabilistic tools with which to attempt a prognostication that can stand the test of personalized time, much less the deeper, personalized meaning of someone <u>else</u> dying. The self's ego cannot conceive of its own death (per Freud) in any actualized way, so the fairy tale of an afterlife has a ready audience ready to buy it fresh and swallow it whole, like children in a candy store getting a special treat because they have been good and behaved themselves in acceptable, civilized ways, that is curbed and channeled their animalistic impulses.

"... science, unlike religion, asks only how, not why. As to the purpose of things, science is silent. But if science cannot talk about meaning, it can talk about harmony." (Krauthammer, 2013, p.117).

Epilogue:
2 poems for the dead (written by the author)

Poem

Trust not the truth that
comes from afar
a smile tinged as a masked
doubt, a foundling at the
door of death

The gap between tongues
everlasting throughout history
quells any desire to sink dreams,
vapid hopes built on false assumptions,
indulgences that lead to a dark river

Built on hope and rumors meant to
bring down enterprise and erase profit
hidden as sacred breath we share,
bury ourselves in the mystery,
the answers run pure and final

Poem

The blade of universal time
cuts both ways
the pendulum of the heart
settles the score

As mundane concerns of a grieving monk
bespeak truth twisted as lies,
moments sacrificed and
desires evaporated

With none of the schoolgirl contrivances
deployed to examine available quandaries
wrapped in extra hair,
extra looks and exhausted quiverings

Now part of the landfill
her arms around it
just below the skin

(The author's dozens of published poems have appeared in literary journals for 45 years, in 5 countries, such as 5 poems in *The Paris Review,* 1971 and 1972; and with at least one Nobel Prize winner for Literature, Pablo Neruda, the Chilean poet).

Appendix 1

Calendar Adjustment is Needed to Correct the Gregorian Calendar in use Worldwide Today

While this section is sparsely sourced, information on how and why the Gregorian Calendar we use needs adjustment due to our lack of knowledge about what year Jesus was born is readily available to those with the right research tools. Further references and sources provided to the author would be much appreciated – contact at scanada@webtv.net, subject line: 'GregCalAdj.'

The Gregorian Calendar is a modified version of the Julian Calendar. It is also called the Western calendar and the Christian calendar, and is the most internationally widely accepted and used civil calendar; see Wikipedia.com. In 1582 the Julian Calendar was changed to the Gregorian Calendar, and adopted in 1752 in England, Scotland and the colonies. In 45 B.C. Julius Caesar ordered a calendar consisting of 12 months based on a solar year. This calendar employed a cycle of three years of 365 days, followed by a year of 366 days (leap year); see Conn. State Library website, 'Calendar.'

Also see www.webexhibits.org; ("How did Dionysius date Christ's birth? Was Jesus born in year 0)?" Also see www.johnpratt.com ("Gregorian Calendar calculated the year of Christ's birth from the available records..."). Also: www.new-birth.net ("The likely dates of Jesus' birth and death; born probably on Wednesday, Jan. 7, 7 BC; died probably on Friday, March 8, 29 AD"). Also: www.calendersign.com; and www.Suite101.com ("the year of Jesus' birth").

It's a popular misconception, based on an anti-historical and inti-intellectual stance that we can't look at the past to learn about the future. Hasn't that been one of the main source of resistance to using the Bible Codes, whose sources are literally thousands of years old? The work required to frame our understanding of the past, in the discipline of History, for example, is not an easy or obvious fit to how we extend that understanding into how we see the future.

Futurism and future history get confused with each other, and many people want to opt out of trying to comprehend the implications of either the past and how it has shaped our present, and how that present formulates our launch from here into an unknown, perhaps even unknowable, at least for some, future. How do we resist our destiny? Should we? Should we embrace our fate and trust whoever is in control?

Even trying to coordinate the calendar with events that occur and events seemingly predicted in the Bible can be problematical as to the year we're talking about, since the Gospels make no mention of a year or a time when Jesus was born. The question of what year especially has been a matter of intense debate, because our Gregorian Calendar is supposed to begin with the first full year of Jesus' life. How might we reconcile this?

The first full year of Jesus' life was fixed as the first year of our calendar by the monk and Vatican scholar Dionysius Exiguss. One day he counted 525 years from his present time (which he knew as year 248 during the Diocletian Era) to the year of the incarnation and birth of Jesus. He then reset that year as year 1 'Ante Christum Natum' ('before the birth of Christ'), 1 ACN, or BC for short. This dating system came to be universally accepted in the 8th century, and we still use it today.

So how do we really know what year it is, in order to see any encoded year in the Bible Code Matrices in context to a time-line we can get a firm handle on?

The Gospels are problematic because they offer two accounts that chronologists find incompatible. Matthew 2:16 states that Jesus was born while Herod the Great was still alive and that Herod ordered the slaughter of infants two years old and younger, and based on the date of Herod's death in 4 BC (contra Dionysius Exiguss), many chronologists conclude that the year 6 BC is the most likely year of Jesus' birth. Consequently, Jesus would have been about four to six years old in the year AD 1.

While we know that Christ was born quite some time before 1 BC, we need to keep in mind that Herod the Great died in 4 BC, so for him to have played such a large role in the event surrounding Jesus' birth, tied as it is to the 'Massacre of the Innocents,' these events must have taken place before or during 4 BC. We can, by the way, be certain of Herod's death by dating the lunar eclipse that occurred right before, as asserted by the first century historiographer Josephus. But that only gives us the year at the *latest*. If we take the Star of Bethlehem as the conjunction of Jupiter and Saturn, then Jesus could have been born even earlier, in 8 BC.

So we cannot with precision know the timing of any event referred to in the Bible Codes that are presented in the Matrix search findings? If our calendar is wrong, how do we know when any particular event happened? Just arbitrarily adjust it within a range of years we can estimate as the birth year of Jesus? That would not make for very accurate history.

Unfortunately, one of the more historically precise indications we have to go on, namely Luke's reference to Quirinius' census, conflicts with Josephus' statement that Quirinius was indeed governor and that there was indeed a census, but in 6 AD, long after Herod's death.

Is there any way we can see to build accuracy into this data that would make it more useful to us in trying to anticipate what is to come? I guess we could keep adding or subtracting years to any found encoded year, and add vigilance during those times.

Before I agree with that approach to dealing with the future with uncertainty, which will probably turn out to be the most useful on a practical basis, although potentially stressful and draining of options, let me recap the telling point here about the calendar. On the one hand, Luke's account places Jesus' birth during a census conducted under the governorship of Quirinius, who according to Josephus, conducted a census in AD 6. In order to reconcile the two Gospel accounts, some have suggested that Josephus was mistaken or that Quirinius had a separate period of rule under Herod. In any case, the actual date of his birth remains historically unverifiable. We will probably never know for certain when Christ was born, or for that matter, when he died on the cross.

We can work out later how such figuring can fit into the Code research results found. But how do we fight the future? If there is a way to fight it, what might that be? Knowledge about what is coming would increase our chances for long-term survival as a species. As for trusting whoever is in control (if there actually is such a mechanism), whatever is coming in our future has already apparently been encoded in the holy script we've talked about. Uncovering it with some degree of accuracy would give us a leg up on options for survival.

In other words, knowing what to anticipate would give us a fighting chance to possibly effectively resist the will behind the intentional actions portrayed in the encoded Torah. While the Books and Reports listed at the end of this book (and other planned by the author) illuminate the fact that the secretly encoded Torah apparently holds the whole history of humanity within its 304,805 Hebrew letters, arranged in an encrypted way far beyond any human capacity to encode (per Jeffrey Satinover, MD, 1997, a reference used in all of the author's Bible Code volumes; see for example one of his 15 websites: www.PredictingPresidents.com, in which all U.S. presidents' elections' outcomes can be predicted using two search result factors detected by the author), we might not be limited to looking at only the past if an effective algorithm can be developed to in effect program the Torah's text to look into the future, that is, decode it in a way that introduces the dimension of time into a 3-dimensionally configured matrix. Such attempts to look into the future would not violate YHWH's injunction listed in Deuteronomy 18: 10-14.

Appendix 2

The Immortality Molecule

The possible configuration of a hypothetical molecule indispensable to extreme longevity might be portrayed in these Torah matrices. Seen in 3 dimensions, the combination of essential atoms arranged appropriately would compose this molecule peculiar to telomeres (the 'cap' on the end of chromosomes that shorten with each cell division) regenerative function that would ensure endless functioning of healthy cells, thus ensuring what would be experienced as immortality, that is, organic, physiological life practically without end.

If death is cheatable, how might we begin to learn to go about doing that? Do some of these Torah matrices depict parts of the immortality molecule, if there is such a thing? Is this part of a secret known long ago by the Elohim of Genesis, those who said they were from Olam?

What particular part of the human genome makes us distinguishable from other life forms, that is, distinctly human? While we share 50% of our DNA with fruit flies, and 99% with chimps, what percentage do we share with flowers or grasses or trees? I can ask that question thinking that we <u>do</u> share some DNA, because <u>all</u> life on Earth has only <u>one</u> basic code, DNA itself. Variations in that code manifest the variety of life forms we see around us in the vast array of flora, fauna, and animals.

In other words, is the anti-death code contained within the Torah death matrix? And if so, how do we go about teasing it out so it sits in plain view in black and white on the page?

In our desire to influence and even control the future, we would perhaps favor the weaponization of information itself – how encoded words in the sacred text of the Torah, if discovered and identified as such <u>before</u> an historical event, could be used to avoid that event. This would constitute a war against Fate, a focused struggle against the dictates of Destiny. If we could develop such a tool to "fight the future" (as Moulder kept urging Scully on the "X-Files"), we would be very tempted to use it.

The political would become one means of deciding who controls not only the decision-making process on target selection and acquisition, but also <u>who</u> has the authority and power to initiate action that would by definition alter history in unforeseen ways.

There is no death without life, and vice versa. With the collapse of space and time (acknowledging the cultural effects of European technological inventions and developments; and homage to Marshal

McLuhan) we're on the verge of being able to predict the future with raw calculating ability alone, that and a knack for naming and choosing the right Key in the Bible Code to search for what main related factors are found encoded in the Torah with it.

Each time that hurdle is jumped we are closer to the grail of knowing some of what lies ahead of us. Face to face with our fate, we must not flinch at the opportunity to stare at the Source, not of course as equals but with less fear than before. These Code findings have removed some of the mystery and some of the mystique of ultimate Being. Each encounter will bestow more Grace and we will become accustomed to walking in that light, reverberating with an unfamiliar vibration, the frequency of which will rival sacredness itself – see author's Milwaukee's 1985 experience, described in paragraph 4 of the *Afterword*, above.

One does not soon forget such an experience. It indelibly lays it hand on you and you are for-ever changed, practically altered into a new type of being, a life form rarely seen on this plane of existence. Your self-consciousness about it slowly fades as you adjust to this new reality of an expanding consciousness increasingly aware of rubbing up against a physical framework of cellular tissue restricting its muon-hadron particle flux of infinite love and expanding hope.

Ultimately you realize all is lost, but you've learned not to care. That's how huge this new love is, beyond the gauge used to measure and dissect and compare. Outside those limits stands the true ground of being, upon which we can learn to make our stand. There awaits immortality, if only we can muster the courage and live the religion of kindness.

* * * * *

Living life means walking the fine line between the absurd and the painful. I can't begin to comprehend what living close to an immortal life would be like, other than feeling the immense responsibility of fill all that enormity of time in authentically productive and ethical ways that contribute to the positive development of life and evolution of society and culture. Faced with the option of a nearly infinite life span, time itself would paradoxically become more precious and pressing, not less. The irony of that reverse psychology of the temporal realm's impact on our psyche becomes suspended in a new soup of unbounded consciousness that would yield to the temptations of beatitudes at every turn, sanctifying moments in unanticipated ways.

"Death is a sacred thing." John Neville, policeman (Tommy Lee Jones) to Laura Mars, photographer (Faye Dunaway) in movie *The Eyes of Laura Mars* (1978)

While we may realize it is the height of hubris to want to live between five to ten thousand years, or even longer, defeating the biological and physiological restrictions on longevity toward that dream might be within our grasp with adequate advances in medical research on extending life. Our nemesis standing in the way of that goal is the main mechanism of death itself, mitochondrial internal cellular dysfunction and telomeres programmed to stop reproducing after a certain number of sheddings and replacements.

Correcting cellular dysfunction would prevent disorders, diseases, cancers, maladaptations, and mutations, thus preserving organ and tissue near-pristine functioning, allowing for continual health and vitality. The new medical technology of using adult stem cells to replace any severely damaged organ or tissue in the whole body is a key to keeping the body alive. Greatly slowing down the rate of telomere replacement is another key to greatly extended longevity.

* * * * *

Life Extension magazine of April 2014 (pp.62-69) has an article about Google's well-financed effort into research to extend life, slow aging, and reverse the aging process, and thus reduce the extent and degree of fatal diseases ... research into how we may be able to cure aging itself by intervening directly in the biological aging process. The Life Extension Foundation promotes the popularity among the world's 1,426 billionaires of private funding of longevity research.

The article points out the limitations of government research in this field, even describing how aging is not viewed as a disease and the National Institutes of Health (NIH) stopping all funding (without explanation) into aging-related processes, but focusing its National Institute on Aging (NIA) on single-disease focused projects such as Alzheimer's disease, which is not the same as life span-extension research. "The NIA is interested in potentially making [one's] later years healthier, but is not interested in adding more of those years." (p.65)

The article estimates that $3 billion invested for a few years in longevity research into ways to slow the basic process of biological aging would result in decreased cancer rates, since a major risk factor is aging. Also, delaying aging would more than pay for itself in reduced health care costs. A 2013 study showed "slowing aging will produce more healthy years than disease research." (p.66)

Some funded biomedical research (such as for 15 years, 1998 - 2013, by the Ellison Foundation) was on "aging, life span, and age-related diseases and disabilities – including telomeres, longevity genes, DNA and mitochondrial damage, Alzheimer's disease, neural development, degeneration, cognitive decline, and more." (p.67). Google's bold venture into extending life by funding research into slowing biological aging could unlock the secrets of reversing aging.

Life Extension Foundation has funded longevity research for 34 years, without government help, and has tried to educate the public "that aging is a disease that can be treated." (p.69). It contends that promising age-reversal research projects need to be funded. It's the world's largest organization dedicated to funding pioneering scientific research aimed at achieving an indefinitely extended healthy human life span.

On March 10-13, 2013 the 8th European Congress on Biogerontology was held in Beer-Sheva, Israel. A summary of two researchers' work is on p.89 of the May 2014 issue of *Life Extension Magazine.* Longevity Genes and Longevity Epigenetics: Nir Barzilai, MD (Director, Institute for Aging Research, Albert Einstein College of Medicine, Bronx, New York) is interested in genetic and lifestyle causes of longevity. He has determined that although a healthy lifestyle may promote longevity in the general population, protective genes are more important than lifestyle for achieving extreme longevity. Gil Atzmon, PhD (Associate Professor, Albert Einstein College of Medicine, Bronx, New York), who is a collaborator of Dr. Barzilai, is interested in the epigenetics of longevity. 'Epigenetics' is the heritable modification of gene expression that is not controlled by DNA sequence. A greater randomness of epigenetic changes, such as methylation patterns are associated with the "biological aging rate." He has identified specific epigenetic changes associated with longevity.

Addendum 1

Author's Note on Bible Code Methodology

I don't interpret the Hebrew letters, they are the alphabet's sounds that match the English letter sounds of the word in any Matrix where encoded words are found by the Bible Code program, where phonetic correspondence is needed for the search, unless the Hebrew word itself is searched and found encoded.

Phonetic matching letter by letter is the process used in Bible Codes to 'spell' the word you are looking for to see if it's encoded with the Key already found. Selection of the appropriate Hebrew letter is prompted by the program's index guide of letters, English to Hebrew.

Otherwise, the English Dictionary of the program will place the Hebrew-spelled word directly into the search list for you. Then it is either found encoded or not. If not, then you can keep replacing words until something is found encoded related to what you are researching.

You do not need to know any Hebrew to do this research. Findings that are metaphorically descriptive are open to interpretation, that's why I stay away from them, and prefer to stay with the literal spellings found in the Torah's encoded text.

For example, I found the names of the two pilots, and the names of their B-29s, and even 'B-29' itself, and the two dates on which they dropped the two A-bombs on Japan, each encoded with the city they bombed as the Key (vertical and letters touching) word found encoded. Also the word 'Japan' (Hebrew version, i.e., without vowels, as per ancient Hebrew spellings of words). And the name of the island from which they took off, 'Tinian.' And the fact that Nagasaki was *not* the first choice of target on August 9, 1945, but a 'secondary target' in case the primary target was fogged-in, which it was. See Book List.

Pieces of names, pieces of lives, pieces of sacred text portray a new perspective of how death is recorded, how individual deaths are recorded in books uttered from the tongue of Yahweh to the ear of Moses. We are finally witness to that intimate secret, exposed here for the first time in human history. Treasure its configurations and contours, for it shows the sculptural shape of a truth we have yet to fathom. Staying true to the promise of persistence, we can honor the integrity of its message and hold steady to what is claimed as its deeper mystery.

To break a name away from the Book of Life and record that name into the Book of Death, the Sacred Word must be inscribed in such a secret and hidden way that it can be a broken text that records for eternity a death that lives on in the memory of a nation.

In an original, fractal phonetic deconstruction, a name is broken into its crystalline alignment with the sacred Word of Yahweh, in whose holy text it reverberates through the ages where life and death are decided by those who have conquered the limitations of mortality, those who intentionally encoded the Torah for us to eventually discover as a reservoir of the Names of the Dead.

Ravaged by disease or cancer, or victim to any kind of accident or murder, or having succumbed to an overdose or suicide, or broken in battle, torn to pieces in the last firefight of their lives, ripped open and ripped apart, taken from life as casualties of war -- this secretly encoded, ancient text holds all their names in pieces, because they came to death in pieces. Torn from Life, their names were entered into the Book of Death.

As bizarre as it might sound, given the numeric nature of the Hebrew alphabet – in which each letter has an assigned numeric value – it might be possible to identify a sort of GPS location for the death of each casualty or victim. In some case, when given enough information about the circumstances of a casualty's death, I have found encoded in the Torah the date and location of that death – these would be published in the full, extended edition of this and other volumes.

Also found encoded in some cases are the date and birth location of the casualty. In such cases the Torah is revealed to function as a data repository of individual biographies, that is, as a Book of Life *and* as a Book of Death.

A caution in this enterprise is how to neutralize the confirmation bias, a natural tendency for those searching for a solution or answer to a puzzle. While presenting the best, convincing case, but in a balanced way, where selectivity does not overly distort the findings and presented results.

Addendum 2

They Also Die By the Numbers – is "Hiding Identity" the Key to Immortality?

There is no escape from being found encoded somehow, even via DNA genome, in the Torah Book of the Dead. While having <u>No Name</u> might protect one from getting killed in a war or dying some other way, names being found fully encoded in all regards (first, middle, last names; even identity as to town of origin found spelled encoded with names and the Key word found encoded) – soldiers, for example, are also identified by serial numbers, usually stamped into a metal 'Dog Tag' they wear around their necks.

Since Hebrew is the only language that uses letters for numbers, in terms of trying NOT to be written into the *Torah's Book of the War Dead*, and thus avoid one's name or serial number being found encoded in the Torah, there is no escape, unless perhaps DNA-only ID could somehow be instituted, but even that genomic sequence can be searched for and found in the Torah.

A soldier's serial number would be found Torah-encoded matching a war-dead list, using a Hebrew letter for each number of the serial number. Please send author verified samples so proof can be published. DNA is also reducible to numbers or found directly encoded as letters combinations of the individual genome specific to an individual. Again, please send author some verified DNA genome sequences to search for in the Torah.

These searches might be definitive proof that there is **no escape** from being found encoded in the *Torah Book of the Dead*. If there was some way to un-link a form of personal identity to any letter or number system, there might be a way to not have one's name in that book. Whether or not that means one does not ever die remains a question to be further investigated. If such anonymity could possibly be the path to immortality remains a project for the author's future work.

Revealing the matrix of life and death ... I recognize the fundamental challenge my work presents to world-views. This is not an intellectual exercise, but involves basic questions of life and death, an emotional subject for anyone, no matter how much peace we have made with the end of our existence. Still, the ego is incapable of conceiving of its own demise or non-existence; thus it has invented "spirit" and the "afterlife," so in the imagination existence does not end with physical death.

From your perspective, my work may seem illusory. Since illusion is subjective in nature, your view-point is necessarily illusion, because your subjective view leads you to that conclusion about my work, my methods, and my original discoveries.

The problem becomes – how to lay claim to the null set of non-death? How to remove one's retrievable identity from the encoded Torah Book of the Dead? If the encrypted text does not "know" about us, because we lack an encodable identifier, then perhaps we won't die. If you do not want to die, do not be findable in the sacred text in any way – by name spelling, by serial number, or DNA code genomic sequence – in the Torah. Might this also include SSA numbers?

Any alpha-numeric code identifier can be broken down into searchable sequence units and found encoded in the Torah. This would apply to organic, physical humans, not necessarily to the identity that might be inherent in a consciousness uploaded to an electronic, digital program analogous to "consciousness." This point at which human consciousness is joined with computer processing power is called "the singularity." Ian Pearson, head of British Telecom's futurology unit says that the rapid advance in computing power would make cyber-immortality a reality by about the year 2050. (See CNN.com. International, article in 'Technology' dated May 23, 2005, "Brain download 'possible by 2050'").

Consciousness is a quality of mind that comprises qualities such as self-awareness and the ability to perceive the relationship between oneself and one's environment, beyond the state of being characterized by sensation, emotion, volition, and thought.

Future death would also be encoded in the mouth of Yahweh, that is, in the text of the Torah as the Five Books of Moses. Whether or not those deaths would be found encoded associated with a specific date or an accurate year of the death is a matter for later research. While such an effort would constitute trying to look into the future, using Bible Codes to do so is not prohibited in the Word of Yahweh. Certain methods of prediction were in fact specified as forbidden by Yahweh (see below, at end of Short Media Interview, on following pages).

Addendum 3

The Hand of Fate

The hand of fate deals us our destiny. Is what we see here a manifestation of that cosmological rule, wherein writ small, is the outcome of a "decision" to end mortality, for a particular individual? Do the majestic hands of intricate time move according to the will of destiny, determining the fate of each individual along the wheel of karma?

To the question asked many times when confronted with these Torah search findings: "what does it all mean?" – you need to grapple with all the implications of that question along the dimensions it implies ... philosophically, historically, psychologically, linguistically, etc.. Do the groundwork of intellectual investigation such answers require and you will begin to develop insight into what is necessary to put such a question in fruitful context.

Given the hyper-dimensional coordinates of space and time, the long-hidden secrets of the eternal *now* can be identified, and revealed in the ancient alphabet that holds upon its tongue, life as well as death within its encrypted language.

The entropic arrow of time precludes us knowing the future; the downward slope of a graph of the dispersing energy advances just ahead of our ability to gain knowledge of the present, much less of the future. The knowledge matrix described by the Torah-Bible Codes encapsulates a focused history of life and death. The bright burning moment of truth shines through in a record of mortality, names etched in time by the tongue of Yahweh, etched forever in the Torah Book of the Dead.

Struggling for control over the timeline of history, Yahweh (Enlil) and Satan (Enlil's half-brother and rival, Enki, who warned Noah of the coming Flood; see Sitchin) do battle on the fields of human conflict, thus shaping the contours of cultures and determining the outcomes of epochs.

The Lord writes you into the Book of Life, and the Lord writes you into the Book of Death – your name as you, at those particular times and places. Your name ... you. As He did for those who died in all their various ways and in all those various places and times.

Unraveling time one stitch at a time, one encoded letter at a time, one syllable off the tip of the tongue congruent with the names of the dead recorded in the Book of Life before immemorial history thought to begin its journey through these regions of fear and loss.

Refractors of the light of truth, the Torah's Hebrew letters also act as prisms for probability, the basis for the universe's functioning. Holding this fabric of reality in its phonetic frame, it encompasses what we hold most dear – the power of Life and Death dealt from the stacked deck of Fate and Destiny. Sensing the texture of tongue and time, consciousness ceases to continue as the self fades and folds into the cosmic fabric we view as death.

A Bible Code search result has something we can't ignore – the truth of it is the fact of it, and vise versa. The contextual relevance of meaning impacts our understanding of our own existential dilemma, especially whether or not the universe or existence is meaningful or meaningless in any measurable, objective way. Subjective meaning might be all we are left with under the uncaring stars.

"The road to truth has many turns" (old Japanese proverb)

If this is all a "coincidence," perhaps (as the saying goes), "It is God's way of winking at you." The message behind the intention evident in the dense and deep encodement of the Torah is another matter.

Through a synthesis of heart and mind we are able to access the archive of what is to come.
Through the prism of a matrix of music we could also access part of the Mind behind this madness, but that is a story for another day.

The incriminating evidence lies in the voids. That which whoever languishes atop the net becomes the light that lives all questions. We know not the path until we stumble upon the means by which to tickle the laughter out of the silent cosmos staring at us in amazement as we flush grace down the toilet of gratitude, voiding the allure of fashion fashioned as iconic cultural symbols of true stardom. The promise of Hollywood depicts fame as deserved glory redeemed at the price of grinding boredom in the desert of the soul that never changes, even for the sake of eon's entertainment.

References

Aichele, George, 2011, *The Control of Biblical Meaning: Canon as Semiotic Mechanism*, Harrisburg, Penn.: Trinity Press.

Essential Guide to Knowledge, The New York Time, 2011, NY: St. Martin's Press.

Evans, Peter, 2013, *Ava Gardner, The Secret Conversations*, NY: Simon and Schuster.

Gopnik, Adam, 2011, *The Table Comes First: Family, France, and the Meaning of Food*, Knopf.

Krauthammer, Charles, 2013, *Things That Matter*, NY: Crown Forum.

Life Extension Magazine, monthly publication of Life Extension Foundation, Florida.

NLT, *New Living Translation, Holy Bible*, 1996, Tyndale House Publishers, Wheaton, Ill. 60189.

Norris, Christopher, 2006, *On Truth and Meaning,* London: Continuum.

Nye, Andrea, 1990, *Words of Power*, London: Routledge.

Ogdon, C.K., and I.A. Richards, 1923, *The Meaning of Meaning*, reissued 1989, NY: HBJ.

Paglia, Camille, 1991, *Sexual Personae, Art and Decadence ...*, NY: Vintage.

Ranker.com website for biographical information on prominent people.

Satinover, Jeffrey, MD, 1997, *Cracking the Bible Code*, NY: Quill-HarperCollins.

Sherman, R. Edwin, 2004, *Bible Code Bombshell*, Bloomington, IN: Author House.

Sitchin, Zecharia, 1978, *The 12thPlanet*, NY: Avon; and his other 5 books in the *Earth Chronicles* series, especially *There Were Giants Upon the Earth*.

Smith, Matthew, 1996, *The Men Who Murdered Marilyn*, London: Bloomsbury.

Smith, Matthew, 2003, *Marilyn's Last Words: Her Secret Tapes and Mysterious Death*, NY: Carroll & Graf.

Vian, Boris, 1997, quote from newspaper article of May 3, 1947, in *Samedi-Soir* (Paris), in Boris Vian's 1997 book *The Manual of Saint-Germain-des-Pres,* NY: Rizzoli.

Wagner, Robert, 2014, *You Must Remember This: Life and Style in Hollywood's Golden Age*, NY: Viking.

Wilson, Edward O., 1998, *Consilience: the Unity of Knowledge*, NY: Knopf.

Wilson, Eric, 2008, *Against Happiness*, NY: FSG.

Further Reading: an internet search of "Bibliography on Death" yields lists of worthwhile texts on the subject. A good study on the process of dying is *On Death and Dying*, by Elisabeth Kubler-Ross (1969), in which she describes the five stages of grief, and the care of the dying.

Short Media (Self) Interview

Q: Why do you do this research?

A: To dig and find the revealed facts underneath the deeper Truth, wherever they may try to hide. Apparently the Torah is encoded to hold the whole history of humanity, in all its facets. I have found, for example, all U.S. presidential elections encoded (see my website, *Predicting Presidents.com*), and 4000 years of assassinations encoded (from ancient Egypt to John Lennon), and world leaders, past and present, in all countries I have looked at. And all British royalty.

Q: Is there related work you have done, such as in the literary field?

A: Yes, my poems have been published in five countries over 44 years, since early 1968, in literary journals, such as *The Paris Review*. I have taught college courses on poetry writing. And at one reading I passed among the audience a small forked twig ... *that* was the poem. A poetic vision is needed to delve into the mystery of decoding historical events such as wars, the elements of which are hidden deep inside a sacred, encrypted text such as the Torah.

Q: You seem also aesthetically focused. How does that relate?

A: My paintings have been shown in juried exhibits in Southern California, and at private showings in Milwaukee and in the Boston area. I like to think my special works in "Mail Art" helped Yugoslavia to break up, degrading the culture a bit, enough to help undo the social cohesion, so the various ethnic peoples there could live free and in peace, apart from each other.

Art is ultimately political, it's not a mirror held up to social reality, but a hammer by which to shape it, to loosely quote Berthold Brecht. I've lived a total of 9 years in Europe, so was not surprised that concentration camps again turned up, in parts of Yugoslavia in the late 1990s.

Q: What other phenomena might Bible Codes be connected to?

A: I also figured out what crop circle symbols mean, and what messages are contained in the huge and complex designs, and *where* the designers are from, and *who* they are. Since UFOs make crop circles, we thus know where those craft are from and who are responsible for them. My website www.cropcirclebooks.com [site now defunct due to hosting service gone out of business} with my 30 books described there is a good start in understanding these two related mysteries. 12 more of my websites are linked at the bottom of the front page of that first site, reflecting the various directions of my research, although more books have been published since then. There is no site that can keep up with my production.

Q: How far have you gone in these discoveries?

A: The UFO and crop circle makers are the same beings, those who encoded the Torah, the Elohim of the Garden of Eden, the Anak of Olam, the Anunnaki of Nibiru, who are thoroughly explained by Zecharia Sitchin in his book series *The Earth Chronicles* (1978 - 2010).

Q: Why do you think the Torah Code technology works as it does, revealing all of history?

A: We are caught in the illusion of time, in that there might fundamentally be not a true distinction between past, present and future. Nature might have invented time as an entropic flow so everything doesn't happen all at once. The Torah's text might be some sort of quantum computer that uses the frequencies of speech sound, as phonetic energy, to mediate manifestations of truths embedded on the surface of a black hole that contains historical information retrievable in the technology of a Bible Code program, reflecting perfectly the projection that is our reality. This is closely related to what Jeffrey Satinover, MD, said in his 1997 book *Cracking the Bible Code* – "... a possible convergence between the Bible Code and quantum information processing ... something as astonishing and humbling as the Code – and the Torah to which it points."

Q: Can we, should we, try to use this Bible Code to predict the future?

A: How set in stone is the Torah as an Oracle? In retrospect, as we look through its lens into the past, we are necessarily simultaneously looking into the relative future, because the Torah was dictated to Moses by Yahweh (according to the Orthodox belief), on top of Mt. Sinai about 3400 years ago. Not one letter of that dictated text of 304,805 Hebrew letters has been changed, according to the Orthodox view.

So in our *past* it contained encoded within it much of the *future* history of humanity. If we query it using a Bible Code computer program, and tease out of it clearly descriptive groups of terms found encoded close together in multiple Matrices – historically accurate descriptive terms – then what can be said of what we might uncover in our relative *future*? Can we use the Torah as a legitimate, dependable oracle that will faithfully predict the future?

People have always been interested in foretelling the future, and have employed many means to attempt to do exactly that – predict what is going to happen. There is a biblical injunction, a prohibition, against such efforts by way of popular means, as specified in *Deuteronomy 18:10-14* – "divination, a soothsayer, an enchanter, or a witch. ... a charmer, a medium, a wizard, or a necromancer. ... these things are an abomination to the Lord ... the Lord your God has not allowed you to do so." Necromancy is conjuration of the spirits of the dead for purposes of magically revealing the future or influencing the course of events We can see the Bible Codes are not one of those proscribed methods, so there should be no fear from the forces of Yahweh by those who utilize Bible Codes to attempt to wrap themselves in the mantle of a seer.

[the above biblical text quote is from the English translation of the original Hebrew Torah text used by the *Bible Codes Plus* computer program available from Israel, whereas the *New Living Translation Holy Bible* uses somewhat different phraseology for the above terms for practices that are forbidden by Yahweh, such as: "fortune-telling, sorcery, interpret omens, witchcraft, cast spells, mediums, psychics, or call forth the spirits of the dead."]

Q: What makes you think you can predict the future, either in a general sense of a political, social, or cultural nature, or in a specific sense as in someone's individual destiny.

A: Destiny is defined as a predetermined course of events often held to be an irresistible power or agency, also called *fortune*. While fate, usually synonymous with *destiny*, is defined as the principle or determining cause or will by which things in general are believed to come to be as they are or events to happen as they do.

So, as I've shown with historical events as they impinge on private lives, such as four thousand years of assassinations and hundreds of years of beheadings, individuals are shown specifically in the Torah to be named with how they will die as predicted int eh Torah, at least revealed in the search pattern teased out conforming to the *proximity* principle where related things are found encoded close together.

Q: What does that mean for what we can say about the future we face today? You even found an EMP attack on the U.S. encoded. Since much of what you found was in our past, can we see into the future using the Bible Code?

A: We can certainly try. The Israelis were able to avoid many casualties when the U.S. attacked Iraq and Saddam Hussein tried to drag Israel into the fight, thinking that by lobbing some SCUD missiles into Israel Arab neighbors would come to his aid if Israel retaliated. Mossad used the Bible Code to predict where the missiles would hit, and had those towns evacuated. The missiles hit only those towns and many innocent lives were saved. Apart from my success with U.S. presidential elections, finding two search results that can be used to predict every single winner, other regularly scheduled events might be amenable to similar treatment. The time horizon needs not be long for the Code process to be utilized in trying to anticipate outcomes, so our task is to try and shorten that horizon up to the point of looking for patterns that reveal what is about to occur, ideally with a large class only but focused on <u>one</u> individual impacted by a universal condition or event called death.

Q: Elsewhere you mentioned the Immortality Quotient. What is that?

A: The 3-parent embryo opens the door to importing the non-death gene so the fetus grows into a person who doesn't die, or at least has an extremely extended life span, far beyond what the Life Extension Foundation is working on for human longevity. In late February 2014 news of a 3-parent embryo broke in the media, as a way of eliminating certain devastating diseases from being inherited, by replacing the gene giving rise to the disease with a normal, healthy gene from a third donor of mitochondrial DNA.

Such genetic material comes only from a mother and can be passed on by only daughters. Mitochondria are found in cells, outside the nucleus, and produce energy for the cell through cellular respiration, and are rich in fats, proteins, and enzymes.

If the death gene can be identified, the one that tells the telomeres ('caps' on ends of chromosomes) to stop duplicating, thus terminating the life of the organism, then we could replace it with a life-term extending mitochondrial gene from the remains in the British Museum identified by Z. Sitchin as the entombed remains of a female hybrid of human and Anunnaki ('Elohim' in the book of Genesis). In his book *There Were Giants Upon the Earth* he identifies the name, artifact and museum registration number, and describes the museum's responses to his repeated requests to have the remains DNA tested, "We do not DNA test any of our artifacts or remains." Unfortunately he died at age 90 in 2012.

The promise of practically everlasting life, or at least extremely extended life with good health and vitality is an intoxicating prospect, and for most people would be worth pursuing at almost any cost.

Q: Do you think you can expose this secretly, long-buried, encoded Word of Yahweh and its implications with impunity?
A: I search and explore and expect no particular result.

Q: Yes, well, what about consequences?
A: You mean eventualities involving the truth?

Q: You're the one who claims to have the answers, so please don't ask me questions.
A: I'm the one who asks questions of ancient texts and symbols. How to listen to the answers is a skill best developed in solitude, without distractions.

Q: Even though you moved to a remote high desert at about 2200 feet elevation, how do you avoid the debauchery of post-modern popular culture, the effects of civilization's decline?
A: I don't, it's a gradient against which I exercise the discipline and restraint to make progress in my research. Don't forget, I'm from New England -- Puritan guilt is a great motivator. While redemption might not be possible, salvation might be hidden somewhere around the corner, so I keep uncovering rocks, literally ... I've done some landscaping on my property the hard way, carried tons of stones by hand. More recently I've developed a meditative hobby of balancing small stones on each other, up to six high.

Q: What Hollywood stars do you consult for about what you found in the Bible Codes about their mortality?
A: What are you talking about?

Q: Rumor has it that some stars have contacted you and asked you to look into the Codes to see what their future might hold as far as what sort of end they might come to, or what terminal disease they might get. Is that true?
A: If I *was* doing such a thing, I'd never confirm or deny it, because it would be confidential, all of it, every aspect of it, even whether or not I'm doing it. That arrangement would be private, and any information gleaned as personal and meant for only them, not for public consumption or broadcasting or sharing in any way. Stars are people too, and deserve their private lives to remain confidential as much as possible. I would never break a bond of trust or violate such an intimate agreement about secrets relevant to one's health and life expectancy. At an Oscars award show one year Elizabeth Taylor was asked by a reporter what was her highest priority. She said it was *privacy*. The reporter then asked what her second priority was, and she said: "privacy."

Q: Are you trying to make predictions in general, or about specific possible events? I see you found the Malaysian Flight 370 encoded as having crashed in the south Indian Ocean, but of course that was after the fact of its take-off from Kuala Lumpur on March 8, 2014 and news reports of its disappearance. No, doubt, as usual, you'll be able to find encoded with that Key you've used for other plane crashes the names of all who died on that Boeing 777-200 ER. Do you have a theory about why it crashed?

A: The pilot's wife of many years left him about 48 hours before take-off, and his persecuted political hero, for whom he demonstrated and attended his criminal trial only hours before take-off, when the popular leader was found guilty and sentenced to five years in prison, for 'sodomy,' apparently a trumped-up charge, would have so upset him he would seek revenge on the nation's courts and legal system, and against his wife for abandoning him. Taking the plane where it most likely could not be found and retrieved would cause Malaysia and his wife enough trouble and consternation as to perhaps qualify as sufficient revenge.

More recently I found a type of natural disaster I had not looked for earlier, about the landslide or mudslide in Washington state on about March 22, 2014, near the town of Oso, about 55 miles north of Seattle. As of March 26, there were still at least 176 people estimated to be missing. The area is well known for such deadly landslides. When I verify the names of the at least 24 dead in that disaster, I'll look for them encoded, as part of an expanded book I wrote on finding the names Torah-encoded of victims of various types of natural disasters.

This level of search results, while conforming to the facts of a person's death and association with the cause, cannot be used for prediction on a person still alive without measurement of proximity and other undetected relational factors not yet identified as indicative of the biographical event of mortality. Further research will need to be conducted in an effort to isolate such factors as part of a pattern perhaps detectable at this level of analysis, analogous to my research that resulted in a model that is able to predict with 100% accuracy the election results of all U.S. presidential races, as described in the book offered on one of my websites, www.PredictingPresidents.com.

Q: Aren't these secrets about death you are uncovering a threat, at least to some people?
A: If you mean the messenger is always in danger, I suppose so.

Q: What means have you of protecting yourself?
A: I don't talk about that. I don't mean to be rude, but I gotta go. Thanks, 'bye.

Selection from Author's Biography

An Army brat born in Maine in1941, he was educated in 3 states and five countries, including later at Uppsala University, Sweden, and Alliance Francaise, Paris, France. He now lives deep in the California desert, having retired early from a coastal county's Social Services department, and devotes himself full time to writing – dozens of books on deciphering crop circles since 1990, and dozens of poems published in literary journals in 5 countries since 1968. He taught school (maths and science) in northern England 1967-68, and has degrees in Sociology. Divorced in1975, San Francisco; no children.

He has conducted college and university extension workshops in Massachusetts and California 1988-1998, including on writing poetry; given public lectures on his crop circle decipherment findings and theory throughout California and in Tucson, Arizona; been interviewed on Fox-TV's "Encounters" (1995), and on TV affiliate in Santa Maria, California, cable access TV in Santa Barbara, and cable access TV in Tucson ("The Cutting Edge," in 2004 and 2005). Also interviewed on various radio shows (local, regional, and Canadian), including "Coast to Coast" in mid-December, 2000. Also on internet radio, Feb. 12, 2014.

More recently, his interest in Bible Codes has resulted in a series of dozens of self-published books. One of his 15 websites, www.PredictingPresidents.com offers his book that explains how he discovered two Bible Code search result factors that can be used to predict with 100% accuracy the outcome of every U.S. presidential election throughout American history, and shows his original discovery as applied to every presidential election.

Books and Reports List

Confidential Report and Book series in which names of victims of accidents, natural disasters, holocausts, mass shootings, assassinations, terror attacks, and wars are shown found encoded in the Torah. All are 8.5 x 11" size, velo or spiral bound; shipping is included in price for each. Send check or money order (in USD only please) to author, Steve Canada, at 1123 N. Las Posas, Ridgecrest, CA 93555, USA.

1. **Concordia Cruise Ship Disaster** – All Victims' Names Found Encoded. (about 80pp, $29).
2. **Titanic's Sinking** and All Victims' Names Found Torah-Encoded. (about 200pp, $65).
3. **Deadly Plane Crashes** and Victims' Names Found Torah-Encoded (100pp, $35).
4. **Fatal Train Crashes** and Victims' Names Found Torah-Encoded (65pp, $24).
5. **Assassinations Worldwide** Found Torah-Encoded: 4000 Years, over 5 Continents; samples, not exhaustive, but many with assassins' name, the location and year ... including John Lennon (about 160pp, $52).
6. **Nazi Holocaust** Torah Codes – Death Camps and Victims' Names found encoded. This is a proof-of-concept manuscript; at one name per page for matrix-encoded, it would take over 6 million pages for an exhaustive illustrated presentation. If anyone knows of a publisher willing to take on such a project, please have them contact the author; (206pp; $65).
7. **Sandy Hook** Elementary School Shooting, Newtown, Conn., Dec. 14, 2012 – All Victims' Names and the Shooter's, and his mother's, and the weapon, found Torah-encoded; including the psychology of *why* (matricide, homicide, rage, hatred); (65pp, $24).
8. **Five Other Mass Shootings**: collected between two covers – all victims and the shooters at Aurora, Columbine, Kent State, Santa Monica, and Tucson (about 96 pages, $34).
9. **Earthquakes: "temblors"** – proof-of-concept manuscript, only *some* of the thousands of pages that could be generated; book publishing contract with a publisher sought; (50pp, $20).
10. **Fukushima**: earthquake, tsunami, and nuclear power plant meltdown, March 2011 found Torah-encoded; only 14 victims' names, of the thousands, were found online; (106pp, $35).
11. **Hurricanes in U.S.** – proof-of-concept manuscript only, that is, only *some* of the thousands of pages that could be generated; book publishing contract with a publisher sought; (50pp, $20).
12. **Tornadoes in U.S.;** proof-of-concept book only, that is, only *some* of the many thousands of pages that could be generated showing the dead encoded in the Torah; (50pp, $20).
13. **Tsunamis;** proof-of-concept book only; hundreds of thousands have died worldwide over the years, so once their names are known, many thousands of pages could be generated as those names are found encoded in the Torah; (50pp, $20).

14. **Volcanoes;** proof-of-concept book; only *some* of the names that could be found encoded in the Torah once their names are known; publisher and research assistant sought; (50pp, $20).

15. **9/11 Terror Attack, Twin Tower, NYC**; victims' names found Torah-encoded; proof-of-concept book, only *some* of the nearly 2800 victims' names are presented here (100pp, $35). A publishing contract would result in *all* names being shown as Torah-encoded, with the name of the event as the Key. Pentagon and Skanksville, Penn. victims would be done later, with a book publishing contract.

16. **Benghazi, Boston and Fort Hood**; 3 Terror Attacks combined between 2 covers; all names of victims shown Torah-encoded, along with the attackers'; (about 50pp, $20).

17. **Afghanistan War**: U.S. Troop Casualties Names; proof-of-concept (about 100pp, $35).

18. **The Gulf War**: U.S. Troop Casualties' Names found encoded; proof-of-concept (84pp, $29).

19. **Iraq War: "Desert Storm"** – U.S. Troop Casualties' Names found Torah encoded; proof-of-concept book (80pp, $29). Later, "Operation Iraqi Freedom," and "Operation Enduring Freedom" could be done as full-length books, with a publishing contract from a book publisher.

20. **Vietnam War**; U.S. Casualties' Names found in Torah Codes; proof-of-concept; 185pp, $59.

21. **WWII City Bombings: Hiroshima and Nagasaki**; atomic bombings of Japan found Torah-encoded; no names available anywhere, except on the two memorials at locations, in Japan only; public appeal for names announced here; all other factors found encoded, including the two B-29 nicknames, and both pilots' names, and even the island from where they took off; 90pp, $32.

22. **Atomic Magnetic War: the Torah Code Illustrated Scenario.** EMP Attack on the USA at End of Days by Iran and North Korea, Found Torah-Encoded. 45pp, $19 + $5 S&H.

Other, Planned Bible Death Code War Books by Author, and Mass Shootings Books:

1. Korean War: U.S. Troop Casualties; later volumes to include South Korean troops, other United Nations troops such as Turkey, North Korean troops, and Chinese troops in the war, 1950-53; and pilots on both sides, including U.S., Chinese, Russian, and North Korean.
2. World War Two: troops on all sides in both theaters, in ground, naval, and air campaigns.
3. World War One: troops on all sides, in ground, naval, and air campaigns.
4. U.S. Civil War: troops on both sides.
5. Mexican-American War: troops on both sides.
6. Spanish-American War: troops on both sides.
7. War of 1812: troops on both sides.
8. American Revolutionary War: troops on both sides.
9. Peloponnesian War: troops on both sides.
10. Other Mass Shootings in U.S., such as Virginia Tech, and the Valentine's Day Massacre.
11. Mass Shootings in other countries throughout history, such in Germany (worst school shooting in history), and in Norway (Andres Breivik on gun-free zone island where he shot 77 young campers and their counselors in 2011); Beslan, Russia, school siege by Chechen rebels, 334 hostages killed, including 186 children.

Other Planned Bible Death Code Books:

1. <u>Beheadings in Bible Death Code</u> – Worldwide, throughout history, thousands have been beheaded. All their names are found Torah-encoded, some with the date and location of their execution. Includes much of the French Revolution and its excesses. And Danny Pearl.

2. <u>Genocides in Bible Death Code</u> – Worldwide, throughout history, millions have been killed in genocides. Names can be found Torah-encoded, some with the date and location of their murder.

3. <u>Death Bible Code of the Rich, Famous and Powerful</u> – <u>Worldwide, Throughout History</u>. How and where they died are found encoded in the original Hebrew of the ancient Torah. We see their secretly encoded *Accidents* (drowning, falling [such as Dr. Atkins, slipped on icey sidewalk in London], burning [Linda Darnell in her house], car-crashing, plane-crashing, skiing), *Assassinations, Beheadings, Cancers, Diseases, Murders, Overdoses, and Suicides.* Their deaths hidden in Secret Code, in the sacred text of the original Hebrew of the ancient Torah. ... a coincidence too far, infinitely beyond pure chance.

Planned Fiction books:

1. 1. <u>Mission to Olam</u> – a series of secret U.S. space crews sent to planet 'Olam,' biblical name of Nibiru, known to the ancient Sumerians as 'Planet of Crossing.' The question is if the Anunnaki who live there will accept these emissaries peacefully, and will they confirm their ancient astronaut explorers colonized Earth (their 'Eridu') and also built the monuments on Mars?

2. 2. <u>NASA Secret Cydonia Mars Mission</u> – goal is to confirm Anunnaki presence and coming return to Earth after their Mars base is fully reactivated, as evidenced by shoot-down of Soviet Mars probe 'Phobos 2.'

3. 3. <u>Brokeback Remake Efforts</u> – in every country American film makers try to make a native version portraying those examples of their cultural icons (as was done of American cowboys by a Chinese director in his award-winning movie 'Brokeback Mountain') they are arrested, tortured, charged, put on trial and sentenced to decades of hard labor in prison.

4. 4. <u>Stars Fade Out</u> – time-y-ons (particles of time) collapsing upon collision impact with anti-time particles; space collapses and devours all stars in a sequence as observed from Earth that the farthest stars blink-out first, then progressively until the night sky is much less populated with stars than before. This presages the collapse of the hyper-sphere's space and time, in advance of the next 'Big Bang.'

About the Author

Steve Canada's filmography is so skimpy it's not worth mentioning (so why don't we just go ahead and briefly describe it?) – a hokey, small western in which as an extra he sits at a table (with his back to the camera!) in a saloon playing cards with other 'cowboys.' Online citing shows no photo of him. And a UCLA film school movie set partly in an on-site desert junkyard of which he plays the owner and delivers memorable lines in a gruff, desert-rat way the director tried to tone down ("Don't do the voice").

His costume try-out fitting for one of the *Planet of the Apes* movies, filmed near the Pinnacles near the California, Inyo county town of Trona, didn't turn out so well – he was too fat to pass for a chimp or human as portrayed in the film.

German director Wim Wenders (over 30 films since 1973, including *The American Friend*, with Dennis Hopper) was in town later auditioning for a small speaking role the author tried out for in a face-to-face interview; didn't get the part but gave the director one of his crop circle books, to which Wenders said: "I might do a crop circle movie."

The author's two minor skin cancer operations, while not life-threatening, alerted him personally to some of the fear victims experience waiting for biopsy test results and get really bad news. He's trying to avoid that through healthy diet and exercise, and extensive supplements that recently have extended into traditional Indian Ayurvedic and ancient Chinese medicine.

So those are his "movies" and "cancer" connections to the subject of Volume 2 of this series. As for 'car crash,' he drove a 1959 Buick off a cliff at age 19 and luckily lived to tell about it. As for 'suicide,' he had a friend who committed suicide decades ago, in Oakland. This is not an intellectual exercise of revealing a secret code in holy writ. The implications are humanly profound and impactful on daily lives.

At age 73, he hopes to stay healthy enough to continue researching for these and other volumes, and also finally do a collection of his poems (published in 5 countries over 40 years and with at least one Nobel Prize winner for Literature, the Chilean poet Pablo Neruda, in *The Paris Review*; receiving an encouraging note while living and struggling in Paris from the novelist Saul Bellow sustained his determination for years), essays, short stories, movie treatments, photos (doorways, stacked rocks) and drawings ('Hands From Other Dimensions;' exhibited at local museum).